ABC Economipedia

ABC Economipedia

Stefano Francesco Fugazzi

Faber est suae quisque fortunae

Copyright © 2016 Stefano Fugazzi

All rights reserved. This book or any portion thereof may not be reproduced or used in any manner whatsoever without the express written permission of the publisher except for the use of brief quotations in a book review or scholarly journal.

First edition: April 2015
Second edition: February 2016
ISBN 978-1-326-24467-5

Published by **ABC Economics**
Website: http://abceconomics.com/
Email: abc.economics@yahoo.com
Cover photo: Stefano Francesco Fugazzi

Printed in the United Kingdom

I dedicate this book to everyone who, during the last two years, has directly or indirectly contributed to turn ABC Economics from one of the many economic publications available on the Internet into an independent and fast growing unconventional think-tank.

Contents

Introduction 1

Eurozone Phillips curve: how the euro affected inflation
and unemployment 3

Using the ABC EZ Misery Index to identify who lost out and
who benefited from the euro 15

Politics and monetary easing, ECB playing tricks on
markets with TLTRO e QE 22

How do forex markets react to the announcement of
QE operations? 27

Sovereign debt reaction to non-conventional
monetary policies 32

Inflation rate in the United Kingdom and Bank of England's
Quantitative Easing programme announcements 41

Inflation rate in the United States and Federal Reserve's
Quantitative Easing programme announcements 42

How will S&P and NASDAQ react to the Fed's first
interest rate increase since 2006? 43
How markets will react to a new Greek bailout package? ... 48

Bailouts, spreads and yields in Germany, France and
PIIGS 53

Italy's tax burden and government revenue since 2000   58

Europe's tax revenues as a percentage of GDP
(2000-2013)   61

TARGET2 imbalances   62

What do financial markets know about terrorism?   64

Sources   74

Introduction

I launched the business news portal *ABC Economics* in October 2013 with the aim to share my analyses and thoughts concerning the difficult economic situation which the eurozone still finds itself in. Over time and concurrent with last summer's publication of my second book *A.B.C. Italia (Abbiamo Bisogno di Crescita)* and a series of conferences last autumn, *ABC Economics* has developed further, without losing its original identity, which consists in carrying out independent researches and analyses that stand out for being on its own way 'neutral', devoid of views that are either partisan or too personal.

The research activity has led me to assess the current economic situation both in Europe and US without falling into the sometimes enticing trap of drawing to a too-easy conclusion by avoiding giving our readers too predictable or semi-conspiratorial analyses, with the view of achieving a widespread success in most popular social networks such as *Facebook* and *Twitter*.

The material included in this publication constitutes the quintessence of what *ABC Economics* really is, a business news portal which is beginning to establish its own place in the world of national and international media.

The author has interpreted the current economic situation from two points of view, focusing, on the analysis of the key economic indicators of the eurozone since the introduction of the single currency (please refer to the Phillips curve and the various iterations of the Misery Index introduced here) and on the reactions of financial markets – including forex, equity and bond markets – to the monetary policies announced by Central Banks since the bursting of the 2007 subprime mortgage bubble.

Stefano Francesco Fugazzi
abceconomics.com

Eurozone Phillips curve: how the euro affected inflation and unemployment

In economics, the Phillips curve is a historical inverse relationship between rates of unemployment and corresponding rates of inflation. Simply stated, a decrease in unemployment, (i.e. increased levels of employment) in an economy will correlate with higher rates of inflation.

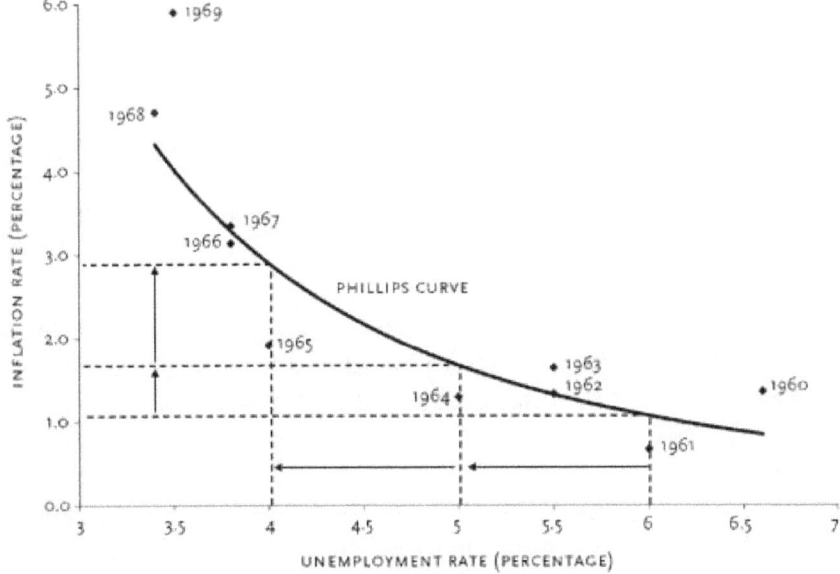

Although he had precursors, A.W.H. Phillips's study of wage inflation and unemployment in the United Kingdom from 1861 to 1957 is a milestone in the development of macroeconomics. Phillips found a consistent inverse relationship: when unemployment was high, wages increased slowly; when unemployment was low, wages rose rapidly.

The close fit between the estimated curve and the data encouraged many economists, following the lead of Paul Samuelson and Robert Solow, to treat the Phillips curve as a sort of menu of policy options *e.g. with an unemployment rate of 6 percent, the government might stimulate the economy to lower unemployment to 5 percent.*

At the height of the Phillips curve's popularity as a guide to policy, Edmund Phelps and Milton Friedman independently challenged its theoretical underpinnings by asserting that the Phillips Curve was only applicable in the short-run and that in the long-run inflationary policies will not decrease unemployment. The long-run Phillips Curve is therefore now seen as a vertical line at the natural rate of unemployment, where the rate of inflation has no effect on unemployment.

Rediscovering the long-term Phillips curve: the eurozone case

ABC Economics applied the inflation-unemployment curve to monitor how those two metrics have evolved over time in Europe since the introduction of the single currency.

In order to graphically represent the evolution of the eurozone's Phillips Curve, we calculated the change in unemployment and inflation rates since the introduction of the euro (*e.g. for 2002 we calculated the percentage variation since 31 December 2001, for 2003 the percentage variation since 31 December 2001, for 2004 since 31 December 2001 etc.*).

Main conclusions on the eurozone's long-run Phillips curve

Eurozone members as at 31/12/14	
Member	**Joined in:**
Austria	2002
Belgium	2002
Cyprus	2008
Estonia	2011
Finland	2002
France	2002
Germany	2002
Greece	2002
Ireland	2002
Italy	2002
Latvia [1]	2014
Luxembourg	2002
Malta	2008
Netherlands	2002
Portugal	2002
Slovak Republic	2009
Slovenia	2007
Spain	2002

[1] excluded from the dataset

ABC Economics found evidence that the original formulation of the Phillips curve is still relevant in the long-term.

Our analysis broadly confirms that in the eurozone there is an inverse relationship between rates of unemployment and corresponding rates of inflation *(please refer to the country-specific curves reported on pages 6-14)*.

In the countries at the periphery of the eurozone, i.e. those which have been most affected by the so-called sovereign debt crisis, we observe a greater spread between the rise in unemployment and a fall in inflation rates.

With the exception of Estonia (who joined the single currency in 2011) and Germany (2002) – within the eurozone, unemployment grew faster rather than inflation, which may lead to the obvious conclusion that the Federal Republic of Germany is the sole core country to have benefited, in terms of inflation-unemployment relationship, from the introduction of the euro.

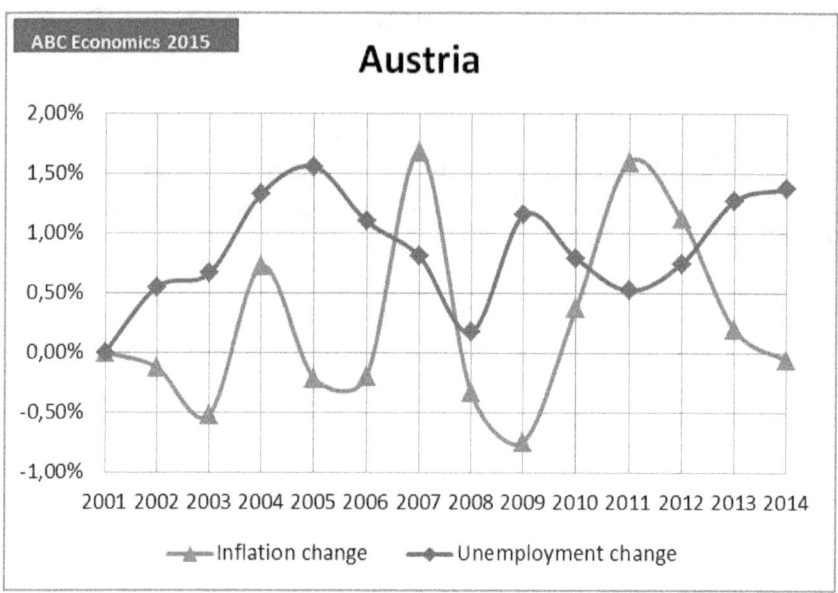
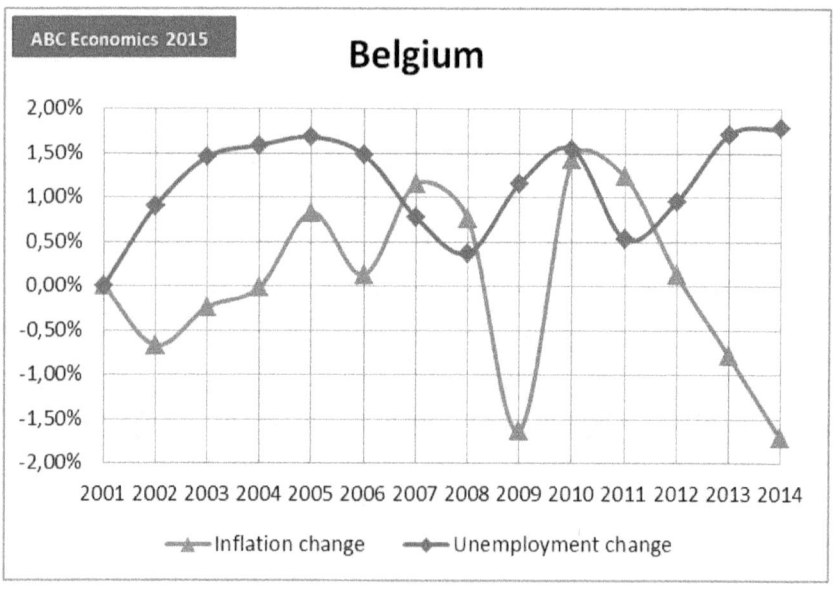

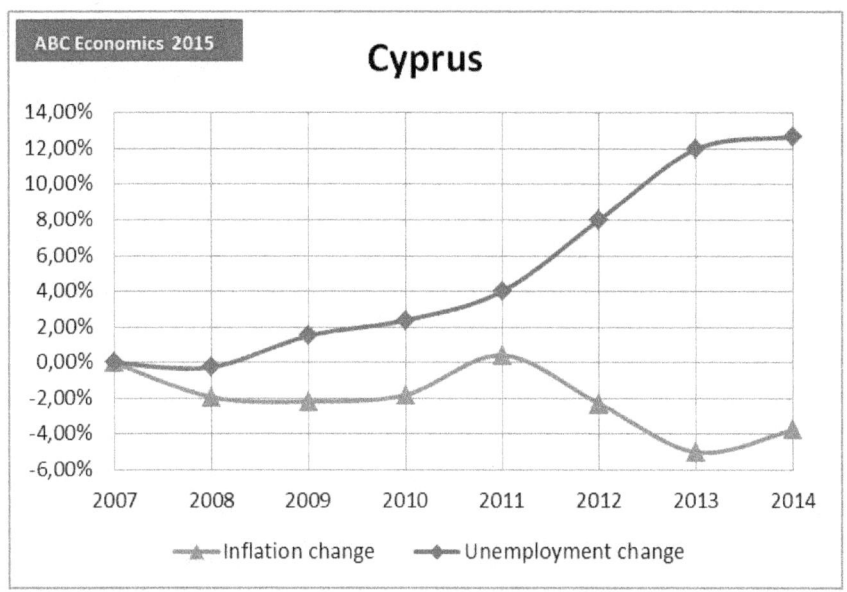

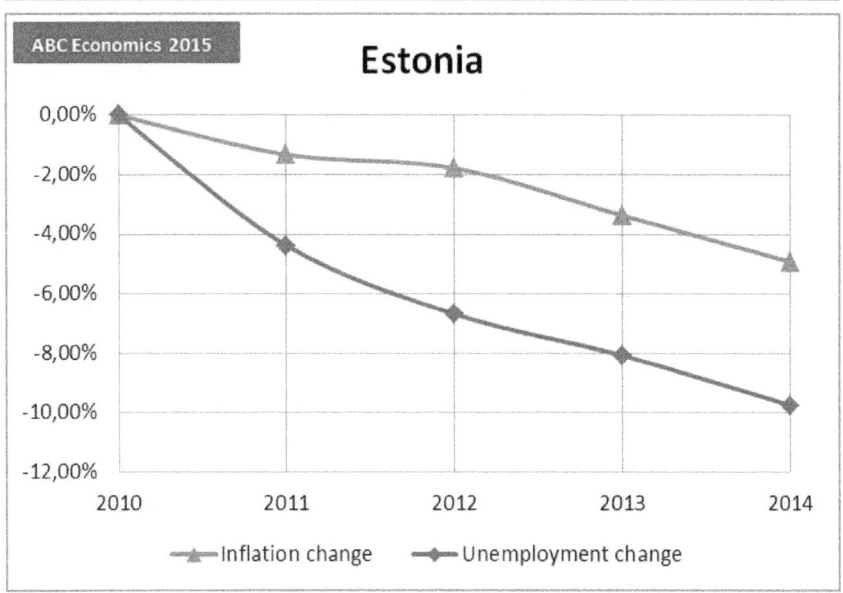

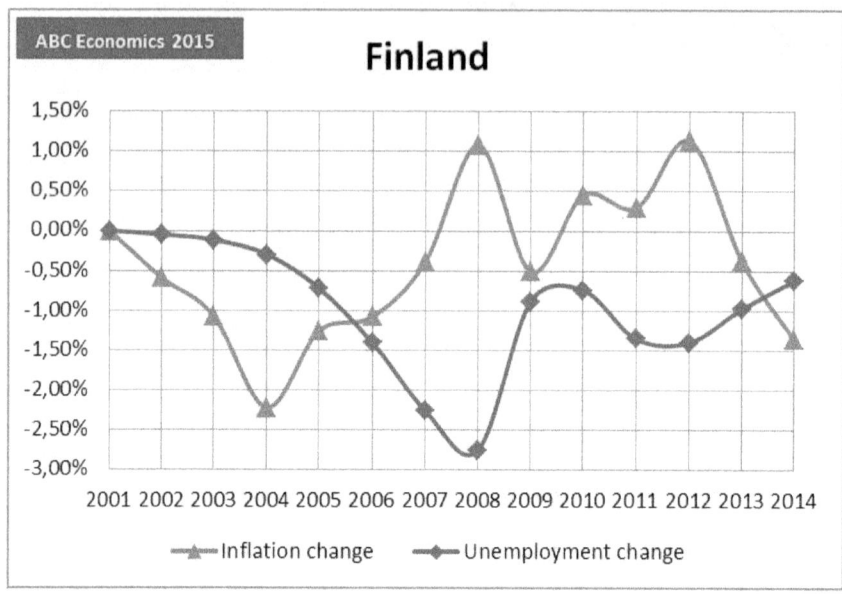
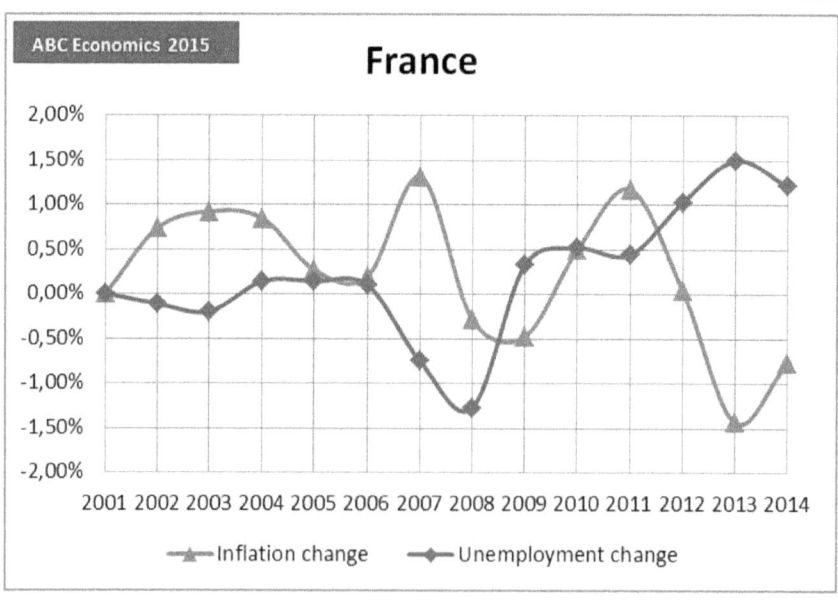

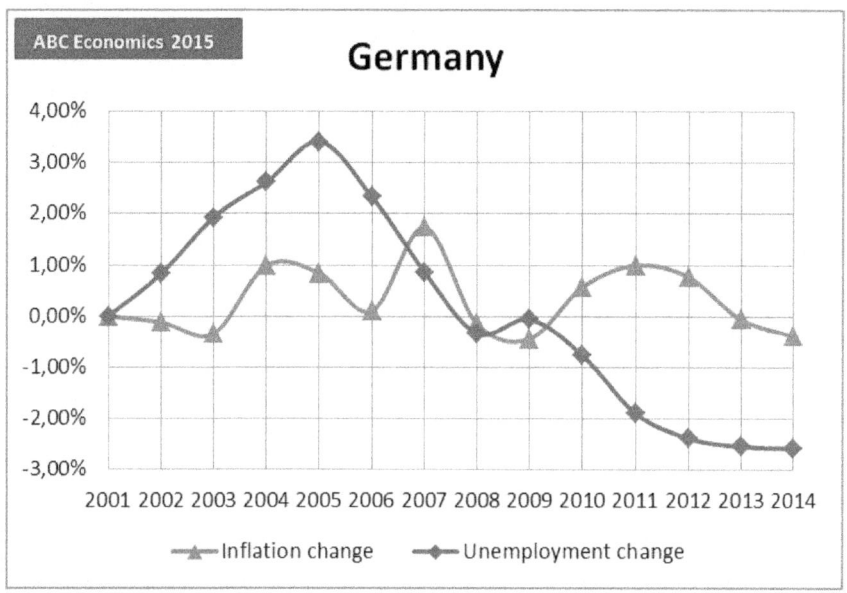
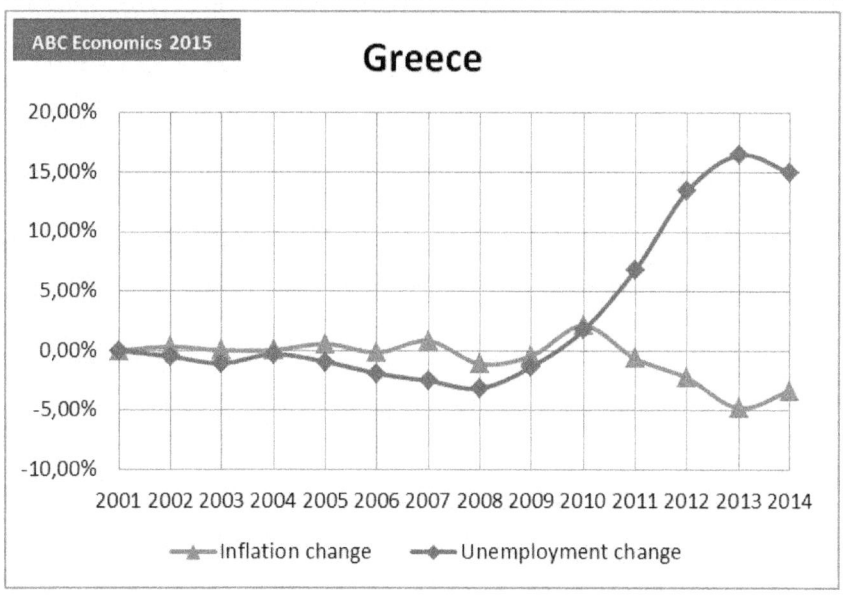

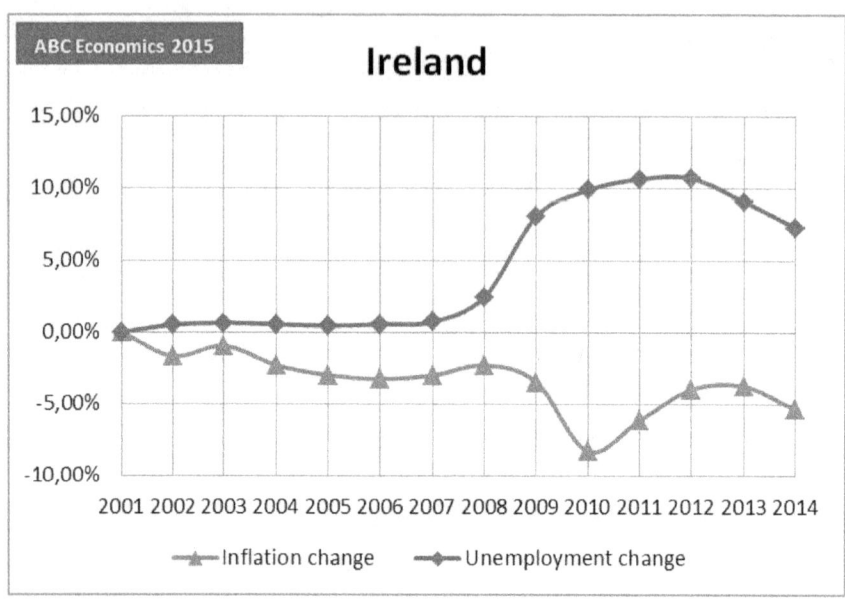
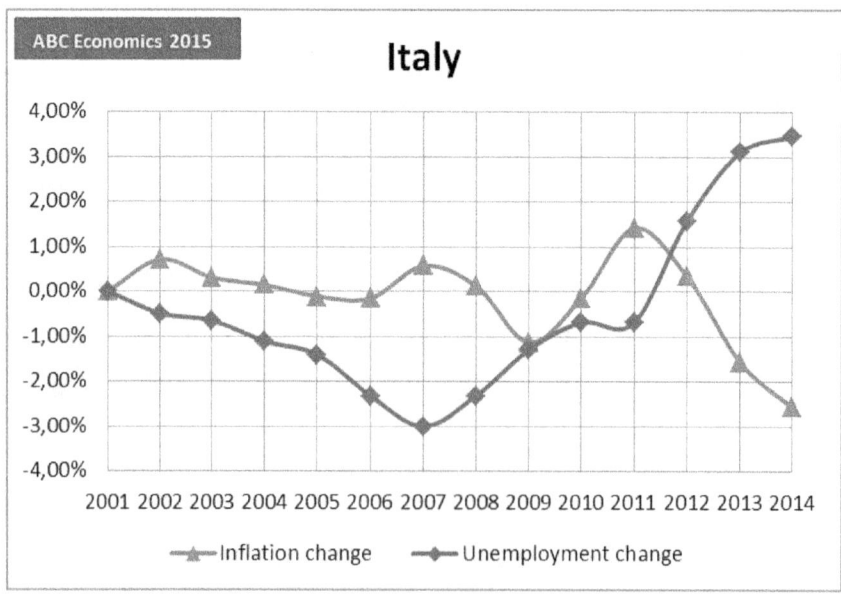

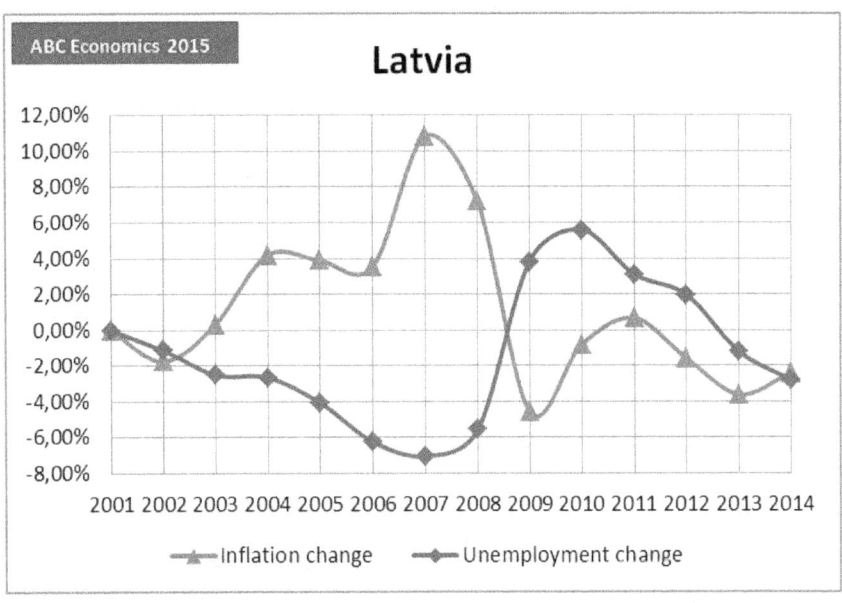
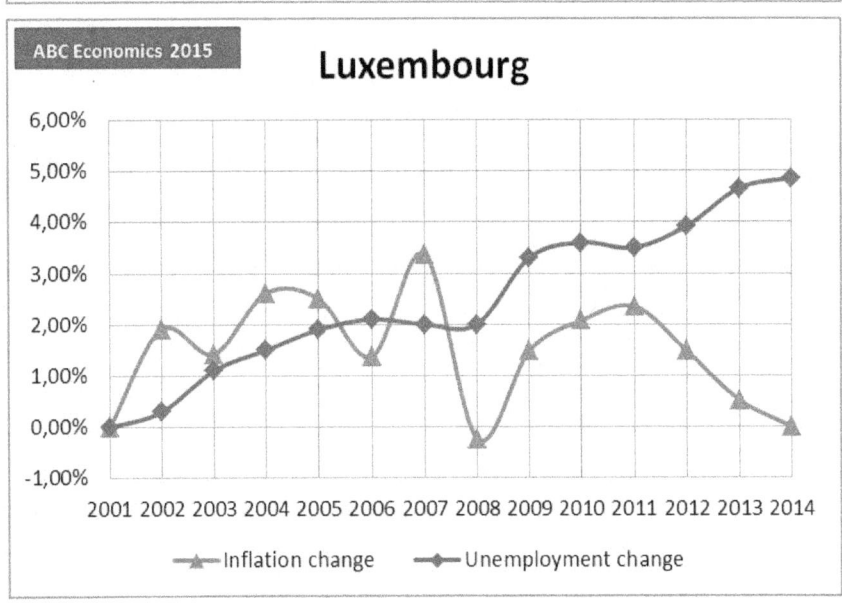

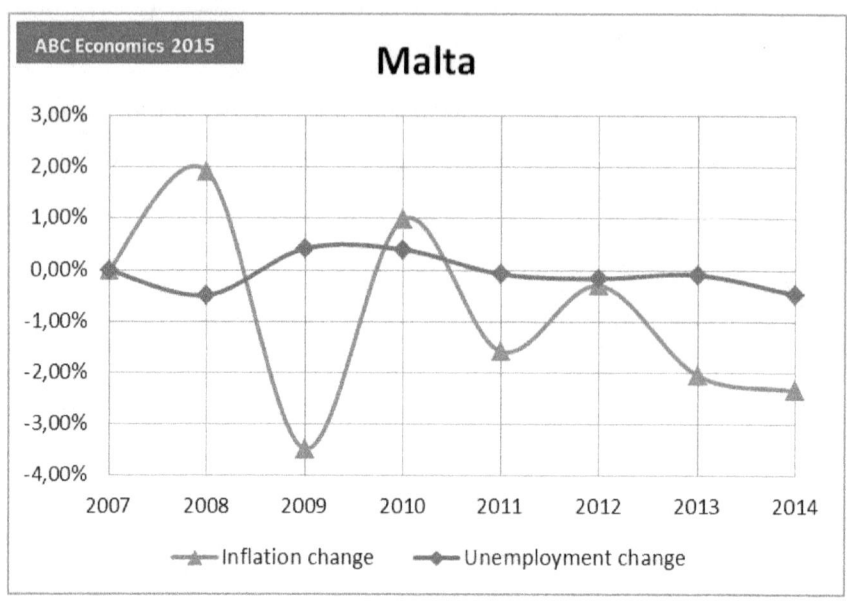
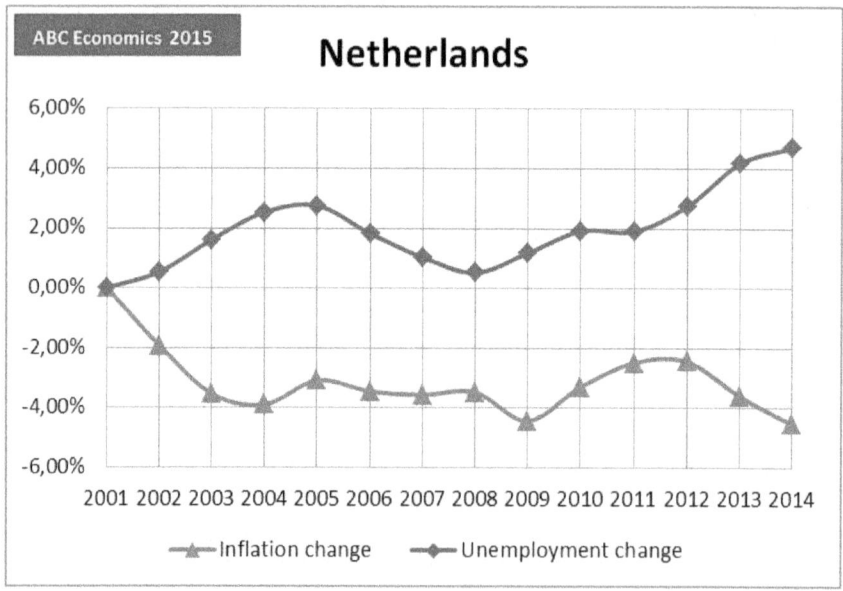

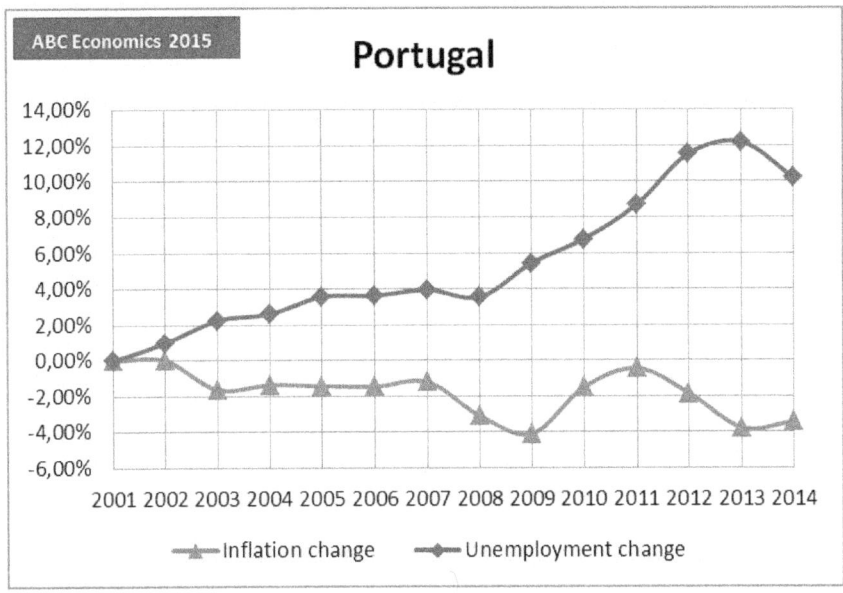
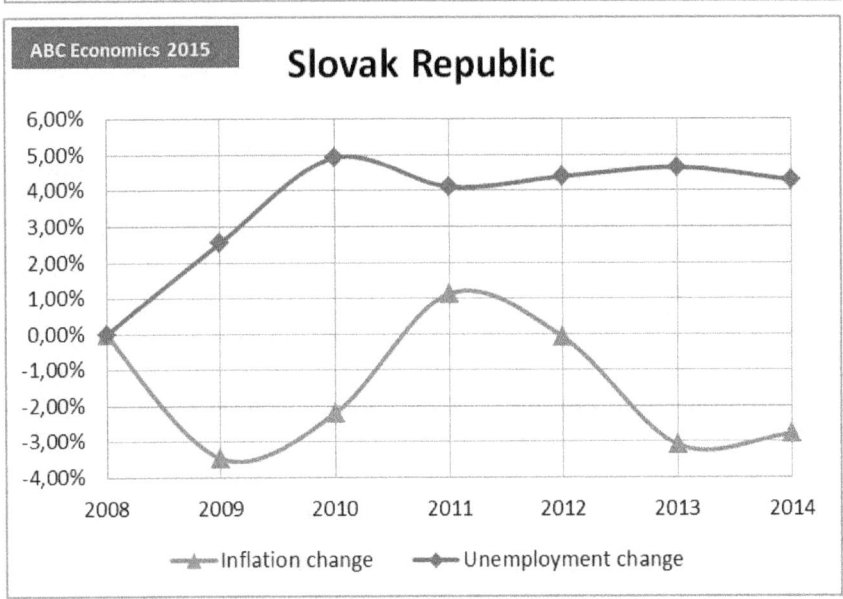

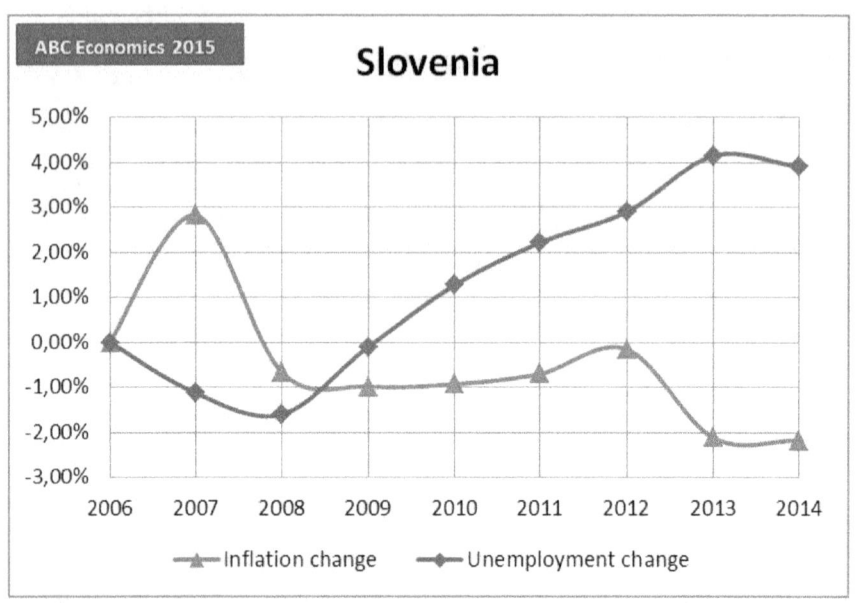
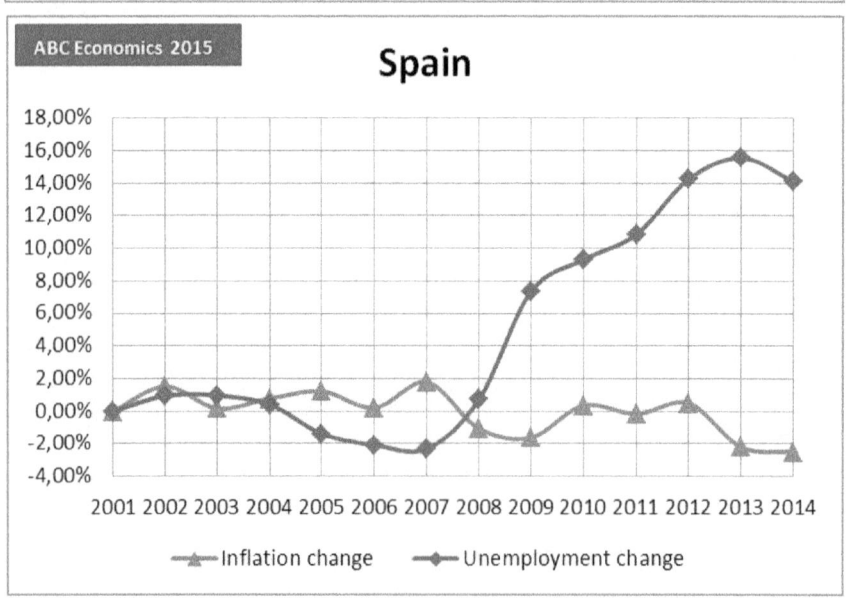

Using the ABC EZ Misery Index to identify who lost out and who benefited from the euro

The Misery Index is a measure of economic well-being for a specified economy. An increasing index means a worsening economic climate for the economy in question, and vice versa.

The author was one of the first to monitor the Misery Index in Italy[1] even before *Confcommercio* (*the Italian General Confederation of Enterprises*) began to track it[2]. ABC Economics subsequently updated the Misery Index metric in May 2014[3] and in January 2015[4].

We have now extended our original analysis to encompass a bigger data set, the ultimate objective being that of assessing how the eurozone economy has evolved since joining the single currency.

The dataset, which features the key economic metrics from all 19 eurozone countries, is sourced from the International Monetary Fund (IMF) portal.

---

[1] Please refer to Stefano Fugazzi's paper published in November 2012: "Italia, l'austerità mette le ali al Misery Index".
URL: http://www.investireoggi.it/economia/italia-lausterita-mette-le-ali-al-misery-index/

[2] March 2013, "Confcommercio introduces the Misery index, will be used to measure the new poverty crisis".
URL: http://www.repubblica.it/economia/2013/03/22/news/confcommercio_si_inventa_il_misery_index_servir_a_misurare_le_nuove_povert_della_crisi-55128206/

[3] "Italia, il boom del Misery Index negli anni post introduzione dell'euro".
URL: http://abceconomics.com/2014/05/28/italia-il-boom-del-misery-index-negli-anni-post-introduzione-delleuro/

[4] "ABC Economics Research: il Misery Index italiano dal 2002".
URL: http://abceconomics.com/2015/01/02/misery-index/

Standard Misery Index

The starting point is the original formulation of the indicator (which we shall call "Standard Misery Index") found by adding unemployment rate to inflation rate. It is assumed that both a higher rate of unemployment and a worsening of inflation create economic and social costs for a country.

Standard Misery Index = unemployment rate + inflation rate

Growth Misery Index

In 1999 Harvard Economist Robert Barro created his own version of the index calculated as the sum of the inflation and unemployment rates plus interest rates plus (minus) the shortfall (surplus) between the actual and trend rate of GDP[5] growth (year-on-year (YOY) variation). Considering that there is no interest rate differentiation within the eurozone, being it constant across the entire sample, for the purpose of this exercise we decided to ignore interest rates.

Growth Misery Index = unemployment rate + inflation rate + (interest rate – interest rate) + YOY GDP variation

Super Misery Index

A subsequent iteration of Misery Index is to revise the Growth Misery Index to take into account government net lending / borrowing (expressed as a percentage of GDP), adding-on contractions and deducting positive variations.

Super Misery Index = unemployment rate + inflation rate + variation in GDP + government net lending / borrowing

---

[5] Gross Domestic Product

ABC EZ Misery Index

One of the most controversial parameters introduced by the Maastricht Treaty was to fix the maximum deficit/GDP level to 3%. Our own iteration of the Misery Index includes only percentage amounts in excess of the target of 3% ("deficit above 3% threshold") rather than considering the actual net lending/borrowing position (in percentage terms), that is:

If deficit > 3%: add-on variance

If deficit ≤ 3% deficit: exclude from calculation

The primary objective of the European Central Bank's (ECB) monetary policy is to maintain price stability. The ECB aims at inflation rates of below, but close to, 2% over the medium term. ABC Economics considered appropriate to include within the ABC EZ Misery Index the spread between a given country's inflation rate and the ECB target, that is the "ECB inflation rate gap" calculated as:

If inflation > 2%: exclude

If inflation ≤ 2%: add-on (Country A versus ECB target) variance to the ABC EZ Misery Index

Given the above considerations on deficits and inflation within the single currency area, the ABC EZ Misery Index will be articulated as follows:

ABC EZ Misery Index = unemployment rate + ECB inflation rate gap + variation in GDP + deficit above 3% threshold
---

Concluding remarks

The four Misery Index variations presented in this chapter (*Standard Misery Index, Growth Misery Index, Super Misery Index, ABC EZ Misery Index*) can be used to measure how eurozone countries have performed since joining the single currency.

Unsurprisingly, among the hard-core EU Members only Germany has benefited to a greater extent from the euro (i.e. the Misery Index variation is negative) whilst Cyprus, Greece and Spain suffered the most (positive period-on-period Misery Index variation).

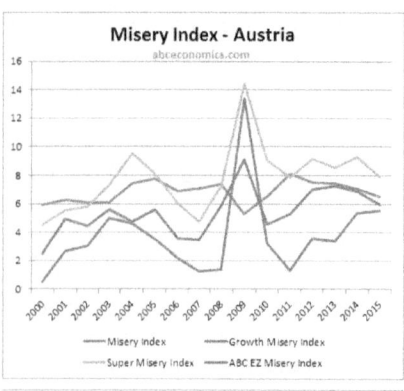
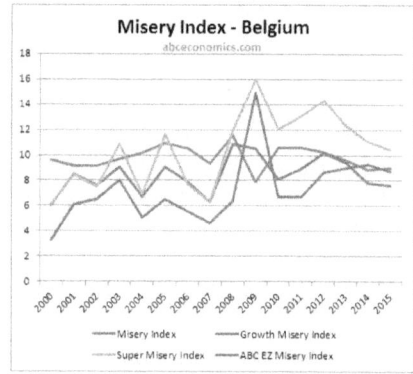
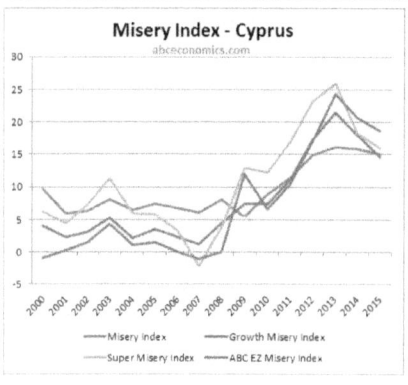
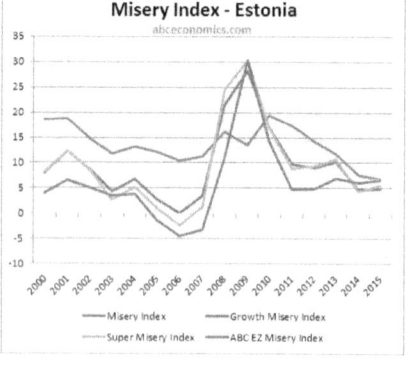

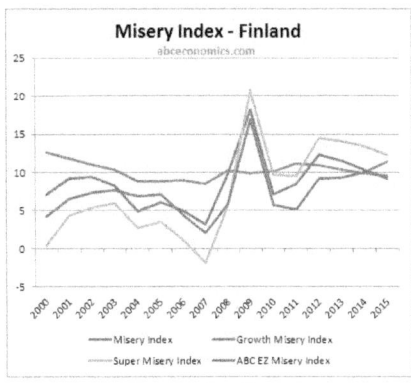
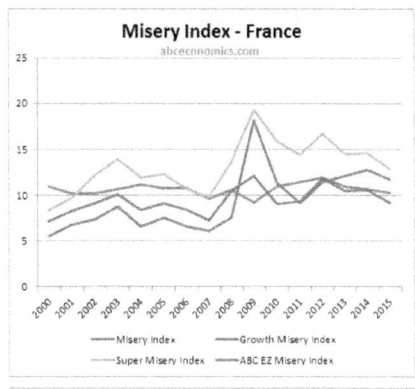
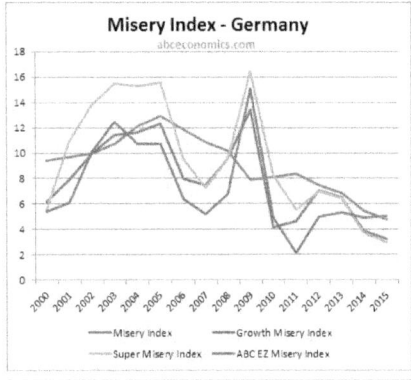
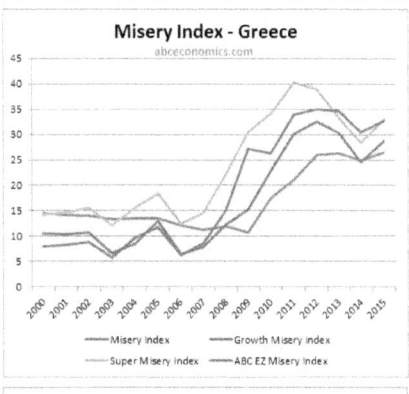
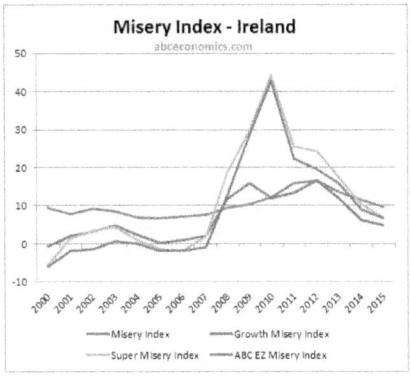
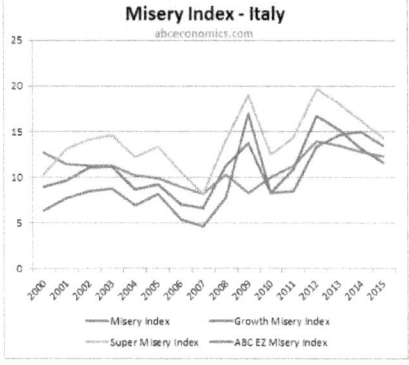

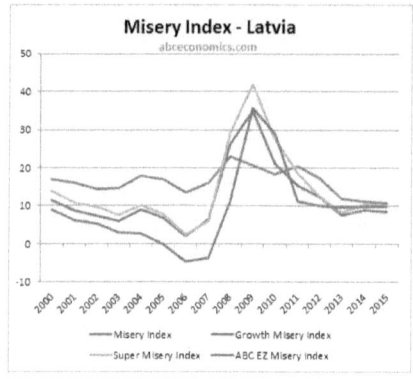
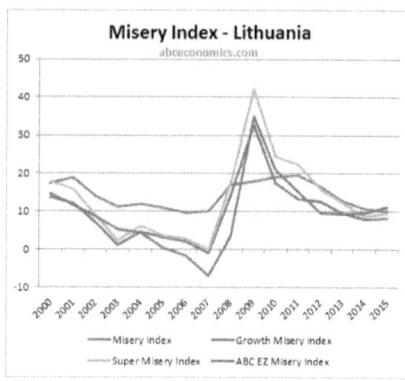
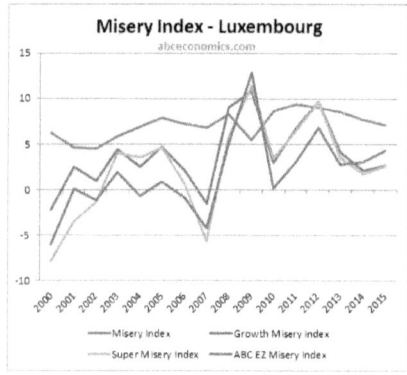
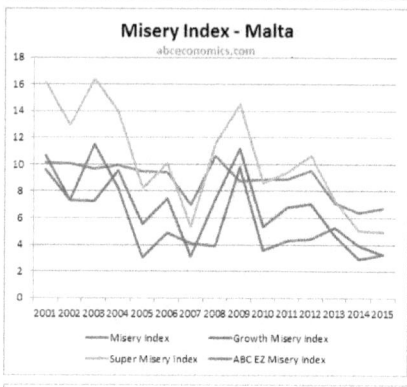
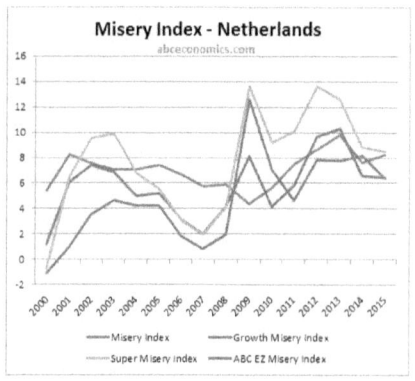
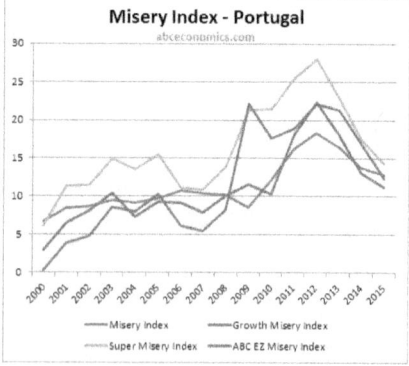

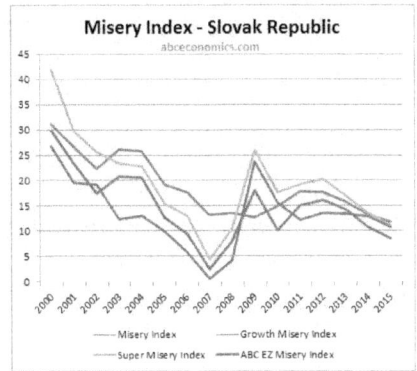
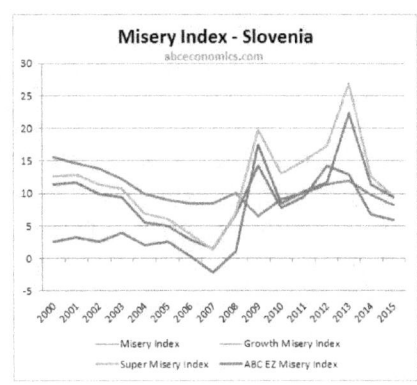
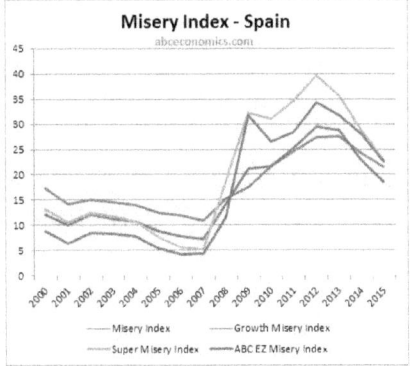

An ABC ECONOMICS Research
based on IMF data (last updated as at October 2015)

For more information please visit:

http://abceconomics.com/

Politics and monetary easing, ECB playing tricks on markets with TLTRO e QE

ABC Economics conducted an event study which observed the creation of *abnormal returns* in the Italian stock market indexes around the ECB announcement of monetary easing programmes such as TLTRO (Targeted Long Term Refinancing Operation) and QE (Quantitative Easing).

Hypotheses

Hypothesis 1 – The Italian stock market responds positively to the announcement of monetary easing programmes.

Hypothesis 2 – Bank stocks generate higher returns than non-bank stocks around the ECB announcement of monetary easing programmes.

Research methods

We collected secondary data to measure abnormal returns (AR) and cumulative abnormal returns (CAR).

To test Hypothesis 1, we benchmarked the FTSE MIB against the EURO STOXX 50.

To test Hypothesis 2, we compared the FTSE MIB index to his banking sector subset, the FTSE ITALY BANKS (IT8300.MI).

To calculate both abnormal returns (AR) and cumulative abnormal returns (CAR), we considered an estimation window of 252 trading days, from 11 to 262 days prior to events. We utilised an event window of 21 trading days, -/+10 days around the selected events.

Observed events

We observed the AR and CAR patterns around two dates:

5 June 2014: the ECB announced a series of targeted longer-term refinancing operations (TLTROs) aimed at improving bank lending to the euro area non-financial private sector, excluding loans to households for house purchase, over a period of two years.

22 January 2015: the ECB announced a Quantitative Easing (QE) programme aimed at reinvigorating the eurozone economy and to combat deflationary patterns.

TLTRO results (5 June 2014)

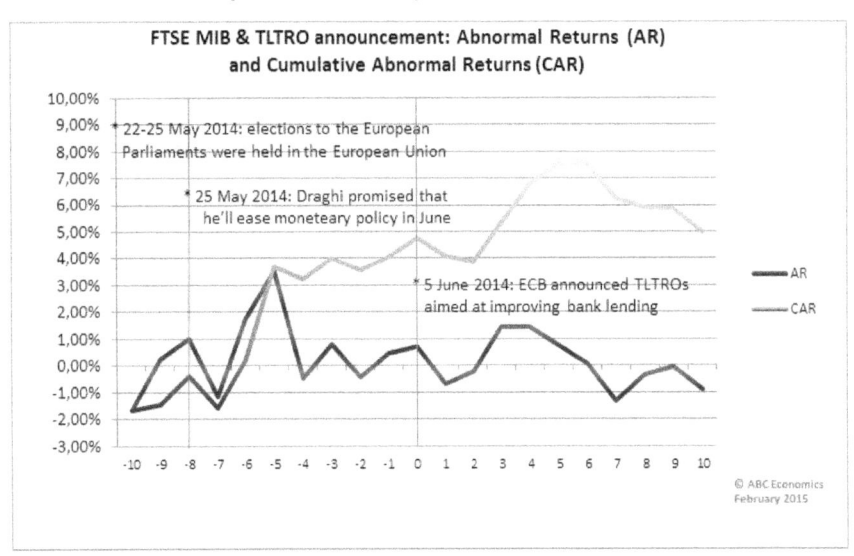

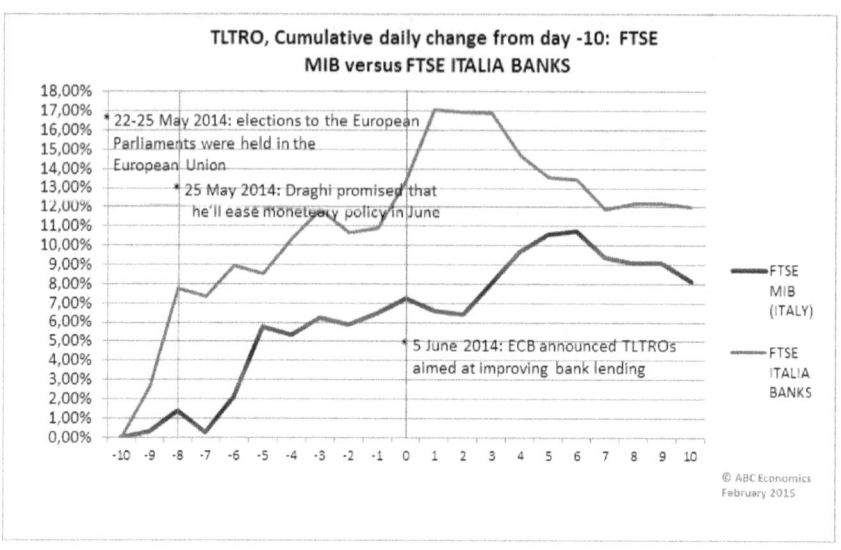

QE results (22 January 2015)

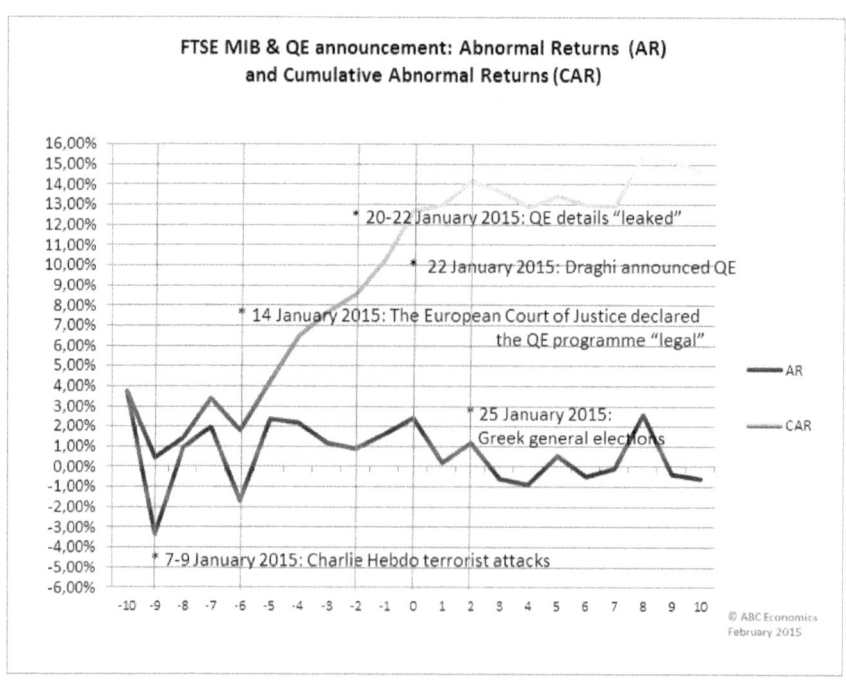

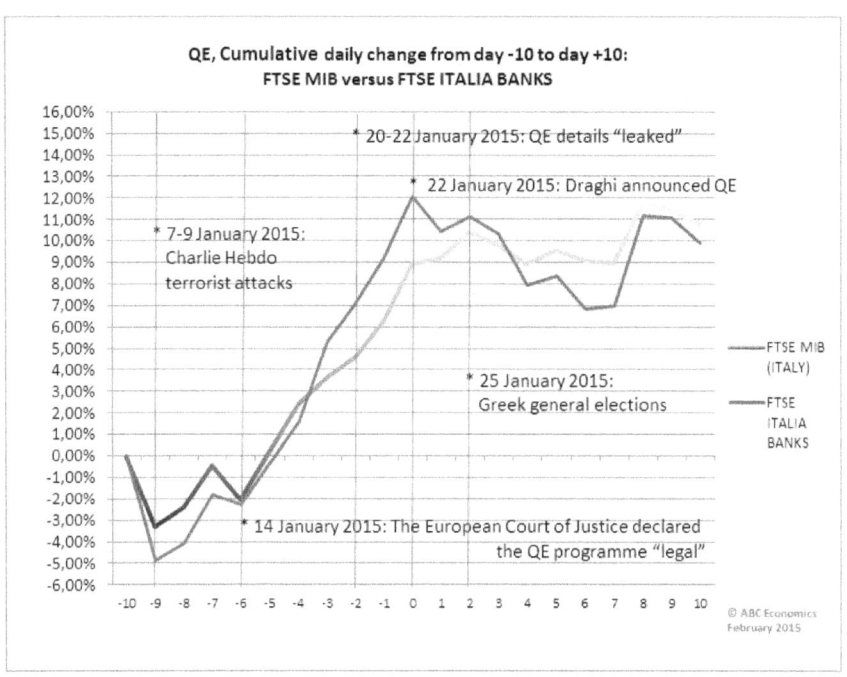

Conclusions

Hypothesis 1 is validated. In line with our expectations and current economic literature, markets have responded positively to the announcement of monetary easing programmes.

Hypothesis 2 is validated. On average, banking stocks (see the banking sector index FTSE ITALY BANKS – IT8300.MI) reacted more positively to the ECB announcements.

A combination of factors, including Draghi's comments prior to the announcements and market expectations, led to the generation of positive cumulative abnormal returns (CAR) prior to the actual events (TLTRO: day -6 and QE; day -5).

We noted that both monetary easing operations were announced just before or soon after general elections with potentially-destabilising outcomes, as if the ECB wanted to take precautionary measures to brush off market concerns.

How do forex markets react to the announcement of QE operations?

Quantitative easing (QE) is an unconventional form of monetary policy where a Central Bank creates new money electronically to buy financial assets, like government bonds. This process aims to directly increase private sector spending in the economy and return inflation to target.

Quantitative easing was first used by the Bank of Japan (BOJ) to fight domestic deflation in the early 2000s. However, since the advent of the global financial crisis of 2007–08, similar policies have been used by the United States (FED), the United Kingdom (BOE), and the eurozone (ECB).

The purpose of this paper is to quantify how forex markets – with particular reference to EUR/USD, GBP/USD and CHF/USD – reacted to the FED's four QE operations.

FED QE announcements

QE1 was announced on 25 November 2008, when the Federal Reserve started buying $600 billion in mortgage-backed securities.

A further monetary stimulus operation (QE2), was announced on 3 November 2010, and was followed by a third wave of monetary easing which was split into two legs (QE 3.1 on 13 September 2012 and QE 3.2 on 12 December 2012).

Main conclusions

From the charts reported thereafter in this chapter, the reader will notice that on average:

- The euro strengthens against the dollar (+0,66% on day 1 and +1,67% average increase over a 3-day period) following the announcement.

- The sterling weakens against the dollar (-0,39% on day 1 and -1,29% average decrease over a 3-day period) following the announcement.

- The Swiss Franc reacted positively to the first operation and negatively thereafter.

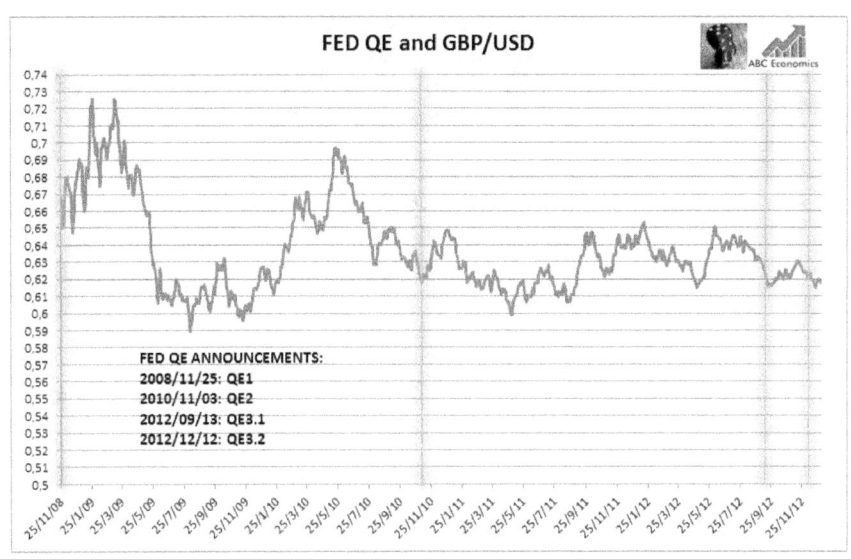

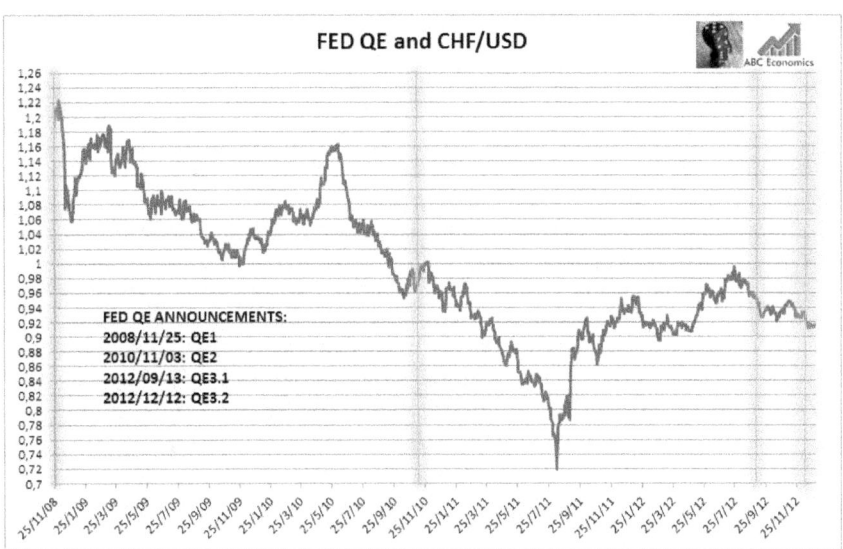

Date	FED QE	GBP/USD	daily change	cumulative change
2008/11/25	QE1 day 0	0,6687		
2008/11/26	QE1 day +1	0,662328	-0,95%	-0,95%
2008/11/27	QE1 day +2	0,653659	-1,31%	-2,25%
2008/11/28	QE1 day +3	0,650202	-0,53%	-2,77%
2010/11/03	QE2 day 0	0,62347		
2010/11/04	QE2 day +1	0,622898	-0,09%	-0,09%
2010/11/05	QE2 day +2	0,619687	-0,52%	-0,61%
2010/11/08	QE2 day +3	0,617971	-0,28%	-0,88%
2012/09/13	QE3.1 day 0	0,622407		
2012/09/14	QE3.1 day +1	0,62082	-0,25%	-0,25%
2012/09/17	QE3.1 day +2	0,618147	-0,43%	-0,68%
2012/09/18	QE3.1 day +3	0,61634	-0,29%	-0,97%
2012/12/12	QE3.2 day 0	0,622219		
2012/12/13	QE3.2 day +1	0,620627	-0,26%	-0,26%
2012/12/14	QE3.2 day +2	0,620037	-0,10%	-0,35%
2012/12/17	QE3.2 day +3	0,618958	-0,17%	-0,52%

GBP/USD	average daily change	average cumulative change
QE day 0		
QE day +1	-0,39%	-0,39%
QE day +2	-0,59%	-0,97%
QE day +3	-0,32%	-1,29%

Date	FED QE	CHF/USD	daily change	cumulative change
2008/11/25	QE1 day 0	1,1851		
2008/11/26	QE1 day +1	1,2036	1,56%	1,56%
2008/11/27	QE1 day +2	1,2017	-0,16%	1,40%
2008/11/28	QE1 day +3	1,213	0,94%	**2,35%**
2010/11/03	QE2 day 0	0,9711		
2010/11/04	QE2 day +1	0,9689	-0,23%	-0,23%
2010/11/05	QE2 day +2	0,9616	-0,75%	-0,98%
2010/11/08	QE2 day +3	0,9661	0,47%	**-0,51%**
2012/09/13	QE3.1 day 0	0,9349		
2012/09/14	QE3.1 day +1	0,9268	-0,87%	-0,87%
2012/09/17	QE3.1 day +2	0,9282	0,15%	-0,72%
2012/09/18	QE3.1 day +3	0,9291	0,10%	**-0,62%**
2012/12/12	QE3.2 day 0	0,9265		
2012/12/13	QE3.2 day +1	0,9239	-0,28%	-0,28%
2012/12/14	QE3.2 day +2	0,9183	-0,61%	-0,89%
2012/12/17	QE3.2 day +3	0,9178	-0,05%	**-0,94%**

CHF/USD	average daily change	average cumulative change
QE day 0		
QE day +1	0,05%	0,05%
QE day +2	-0,34%	-0,29%
QE day +3	0,36%	0,07%

ABC Economics

Sovereign debt reaction to non-conventional monetary policies

In this chapter we assess the sovereign debt market's reaction to the ECB announcement of non-conventional monetary policies. With that in mind, we selected the following policy announcements:

- 7 May 2009: Covered Bond Purchase Programme (CBPP)
- 10 May 2010: Securities Markets Programme (SMP)
- 6 October 2011: Long Term Refinancing Operation (LTRO)
- 2 August 2012: Outright Monetary Transactions (OMT)
- 5 June 2014: Targeted Longer Term Refinancing Operations (TLTRO)
- 22 January 2015: Quantitative Easing (QE)

To derive the variations in yields, we selected the 10-year sovereign papers of France, Germany, Greece, Ireland, Italy, Portugal and Spain.

Main conclusions

In the cases of the announcement of the CBPP and LTRO programmes, within the 0-3 days horizon, we noticed a yield increase across the entire sample reaching a +7.73% in the case of Germany's bunds following the Long Term Refinancing Operation. A similar pattern was also observed within the day -3 to day +3 horizon with highs of +15.47% and 12.50% for France and Germany following the announcement of the LTRO, with the exceptions of Irish,

Greek and Portuguese papers whose yields declined by 2-3% in the case of the CBBP.

Percentage movement in 10-year government bonds following Ecb monetary policy announcements

CBPP

	Germany	France	Portugal	Italy	Ireland	Greece	Spain
Change on announcement day	4,31%	3,87%	0,75%	0,96%	-0,78%	-2,20%	2,55%
Day -1 to day +1 change	6,15%	4,97%	1,26%	1,20%	-0,98%	-2,99%	2,81%
Day -3 to day +3 change	7,23%	5,87%	-2,43%	1,91%	-1,54%	-2,73%	3,07%
Day 0 to day +3 change	0,59%	0,80%	0,25%	1,91%	0,79%	1,63%	0,25%

SMP

	Germany	France	Portugal	Italy	Ireland	Greece	Spain
Change on announcement day	5,45%	2,87%	-26,53%	-7,48%	-18,03%	-36,29%	-10,91%
Day -1 to day +1 change	4,36%	2,23%	-28,41%	-7,24%	-20,87%	-39,22%	-10,23%
Day -3 to day +3 change	2,86%	1,27%	-23,34%	-0,76%	-18,02%	-28,00%	-6,24%
Day 0 to day +3 change	-0,69%	-1,55%	-3,85%	-0,51%	-5,50%	-6,39%	-0,26%

LTRO

	Germany	France	Portugal	Italy	Ireland	Greece	Spain
Change on announcement day	5,43%	3,01%	0,90%	-1,45%	1,21%	1,07%	-1,58%
Day -1 to day +1 change	8,70%	3,38%	0,90%	-0,36%	0,54%	-0,67%	-1,97%
Day -3 to day +3 change	15,47%	12,50%	3,30%	1,63%	6,55%	4,44%	-2,16%
Day 0 to day +3 change	7,73%	5,11%	1,38%	2,94%	5,84%	0,31%	0,00%

A green light identifies a percentage reduction in yields, an amber light an increase up to 5%, a red light movements over +5%

ABC Economics Research

Percentage movement in 10-year government bonds following Ecb monetary policy announcements

OMT

	Germany	France	Portugal	Italy	Ireland	Greece	Spain
Change on announcement day	-10,22%	-1,91%	-2,15%	6,24%	N/A	1,08%	5,85%
Day -1 to day +1 change	3,65%	0,96%	-1,87%	2,19%	N/A	-0,95%	2,25%
Day -3 to day +3 change	8,03%	-0,46%	-10,78%	0,17%	N/A	-3,23%	3,34%
Day 0 to day +3 change	20,33%	4,88%	-7,55%	-5,40%	N/A	-5,67%	-3,68%

TLTRO

	Germany	France	Portugal	Italy	Ireland	Greece	Spain
Change on announcement day	-2,10%	-2,70%	-0,82%	-2,98%	-1,91%	-2,53%	-2,09%
Day -1 to day +1 change	-5,59%	-7,57%	-4,37%	-9,27%	-7,25%	-9,64%	-8,01%
Day -3 to day +3 change	2,19%	-0,56%	-9,04%	-5,74%	-6,61%	-10,66%	-7,75%
Day 0 to day +3 change	0,00%	-2,22%	-8,54%	-4,78%	-6,61%	-10,37%	-6,76%

QE

	Germany	France	Portugal	Italy	Ireland	Greece	Spain
Change on announcement day	-17,02%	-11,43%	-7,57%	-7,74%	-9,35%	-4,56%	-9,03%
Day -1 to day +1 change	-31,91%	-22,86%	-12,35%	-10,71%	-15,89%	-10,21%	-12,90%
Day -3 to day +3 change	-12,82%	-7,94%	-10,12%	-9,58%	-5,94%	2,38%	-7,95%
Day 0 to day +3 change	-12,82%	-6,45%	-4,31%	-2,58%	-2,06%	7,85%	-1,42%

A green light identifies a percentage reduction in yields, an amber light an increase up to 5%, a red light movements over +5%

ABC Economics Research

The announcement of SMP, TLTRO and QE operations have led to an overall decrease of yields over the day 0 to day +3 horizon, with the sole exception of Greece where the ECB has opted not to include the Hellenic country within the latest monetary programme.

Mixed reactions for the OMT which was intended as a replacement for the SMP. Negative for France and Germany (an increase in the 10-year yields) and positive for the PIIGS (Portugal, Italy, Greece and Portugal) countries (a decrease in yields).

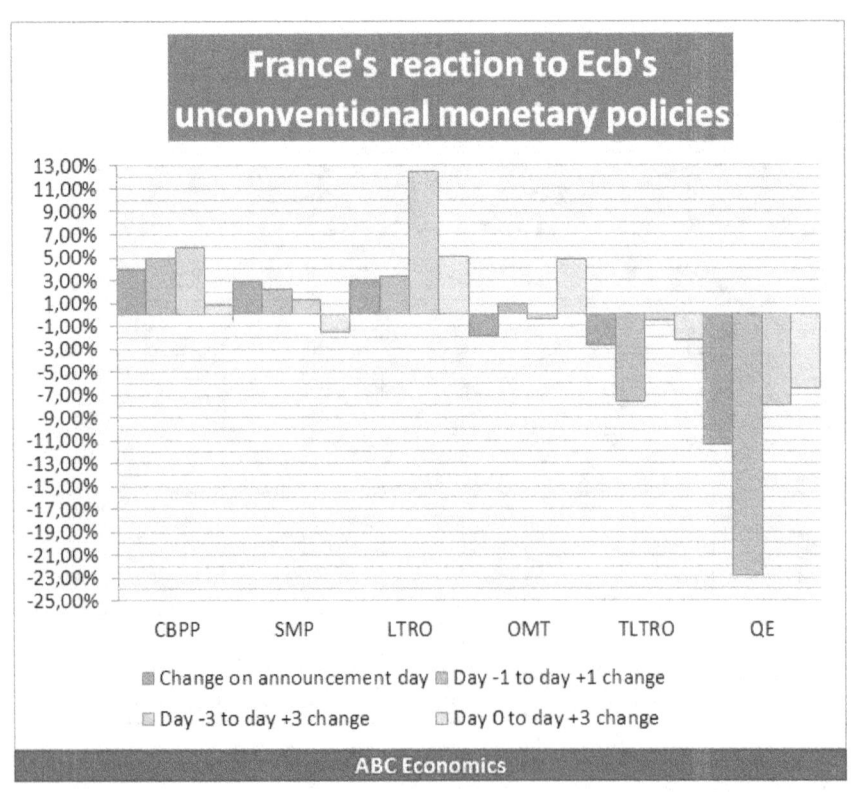

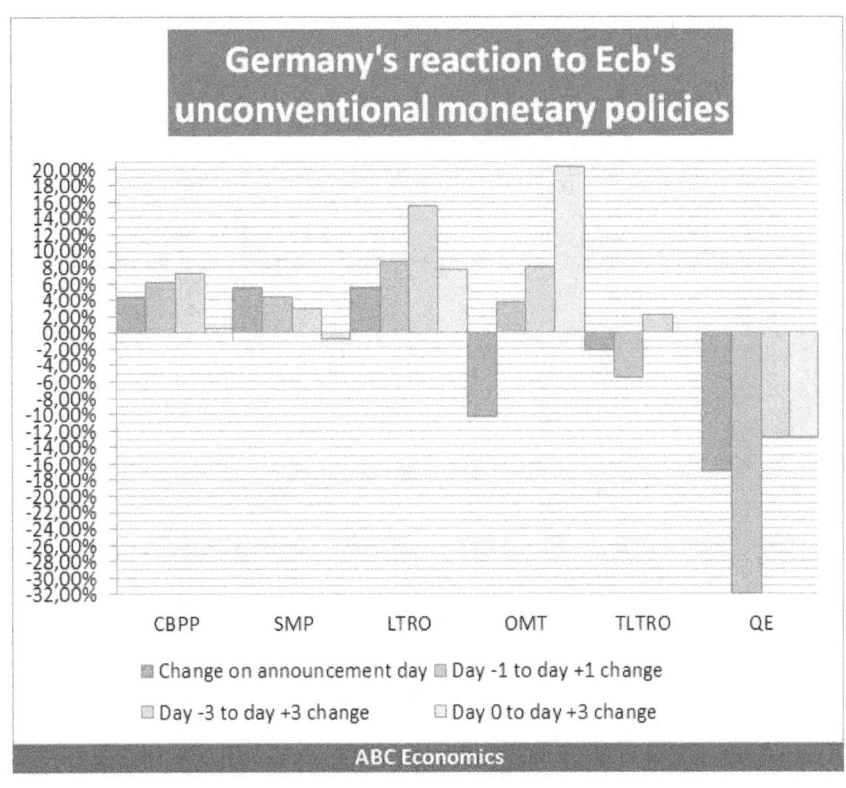

Notes on non-conventional monetary policies

The Covered Bond Purchase Programme (**CBPP**) was a programme announced on 7 May 2009 on the basis of article 18 of the ECB statute. It has been in operation during two periods. The ECB first intervened between July 2009 and June 2010 (CBPP1), during which time the ECB outright purchased 60 billion euro of covered bonds. On 6 October 2011 the ECB announced it would reactivate the programme (CBPP2) and that it was intended to amount to 40 billion euro between November 2011 and October 2012. On 3 November 2011 the ECB announced further details about maturities, eligibility and counterparties.

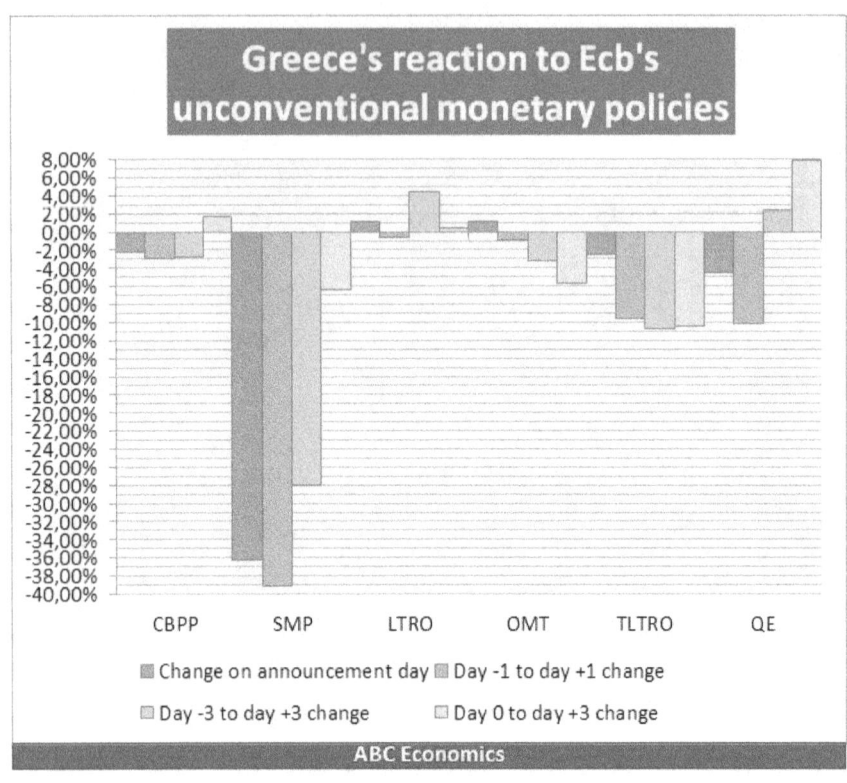

The **SMP** program was initiated in May 2010 as part of the euro-system's single monetary policy. It was intended as a temporary program to address malfunctioning in the securities markets and to allow the normal functioning of the monetary policy transmission mechanism. The interventions were sterilised as equivalent liquidity was withdrawn from the system by the ECB to leave the SMP monetary policy "neutral". There was no monetisation of eurozone sovereign debt. Liquidity was absorbed by the ECB via the collection of 1-week fixed term deposits.

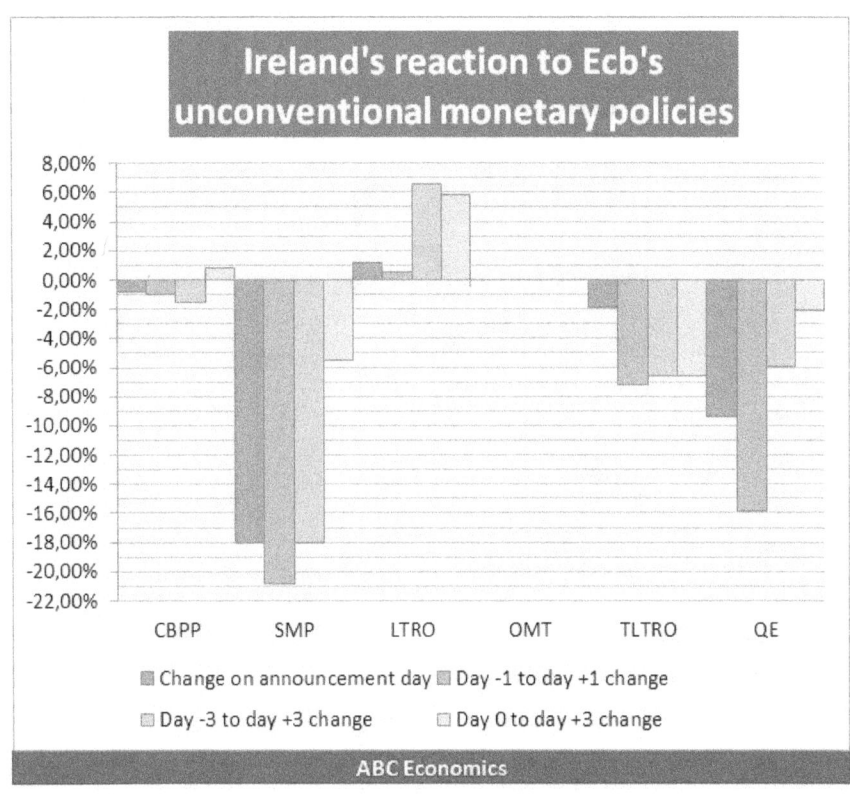

The European Central Bank's long-term refinancing operation was a process by which the ECB provided financing to eurozone banks. The stated aim of the **LTRO** was to maintain a cushion of liquidity for banks holding illiquid assets, and thus prevent interbank lending and other loan origination from seizing up as they did in the credit squeeze of 2008.

Outright Monetary Transactions (**OMT**) was a program of the European Central Bank under which the bank made purchases ("outright transactions") in secondary, sovereign bond markets, under certain conditions, of bonds issued by eurozone member-states.

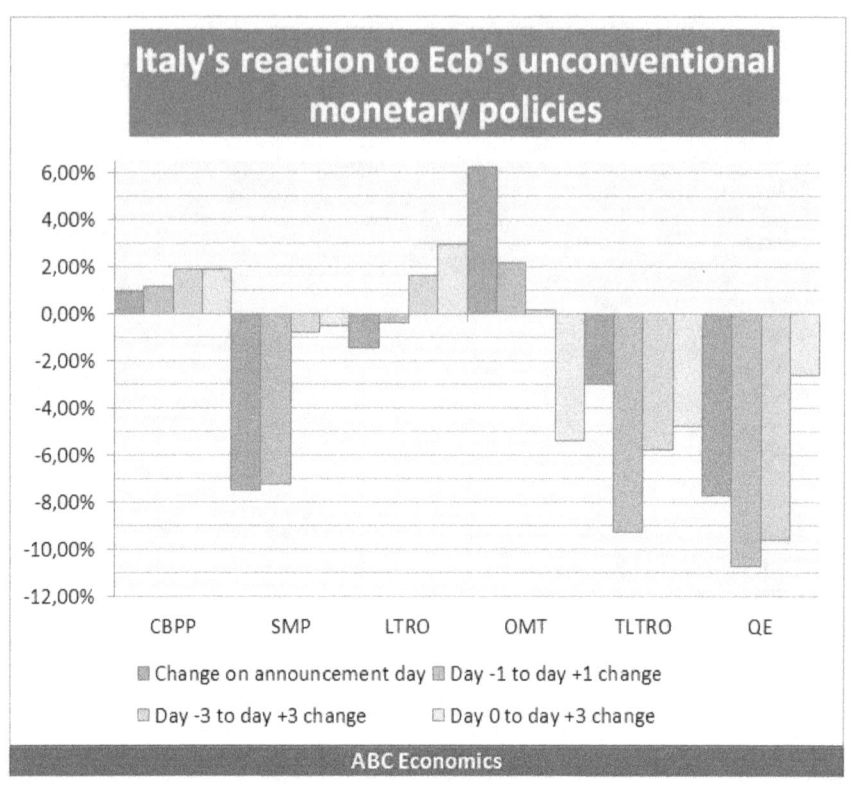

In pursuing its price stability mandate, the Governing Council of the ECB announced measures to enhance the functioning of the monetary policy transmission mechanism by supporting lending to the real economy. In particular, the Governing Council decided to conduct a series of targeted longer-term refinancing operations (**TLTROs**) aimed at improving bank lending to the euro area non-financial private sector, excluding loans to households for house purchase, over a window of two years.

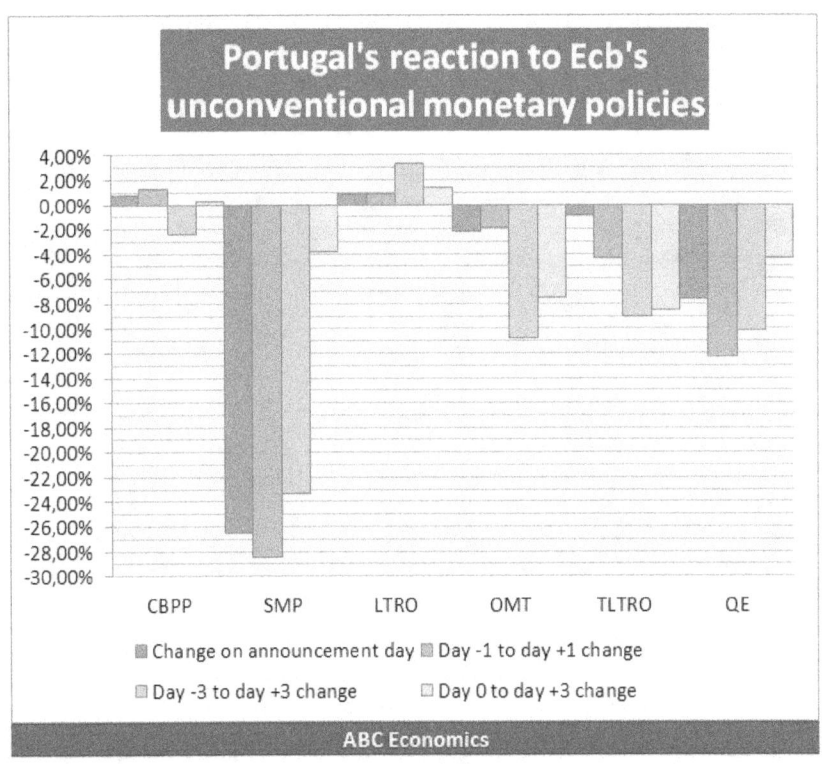

QE – In March 2015 the ECB and national central banks of eurozone member states started buying 60 billion euro of government debt each month. That figure included re-bundled private debt, asset-backed securities and covered bonds, typically worth about 10 billion euro, on top of the roughly 50 billion euro in state bonds. The programme will run until September 2016 or until there has been a "sustained" improvement in consumer price inflation, which recently turned negative.

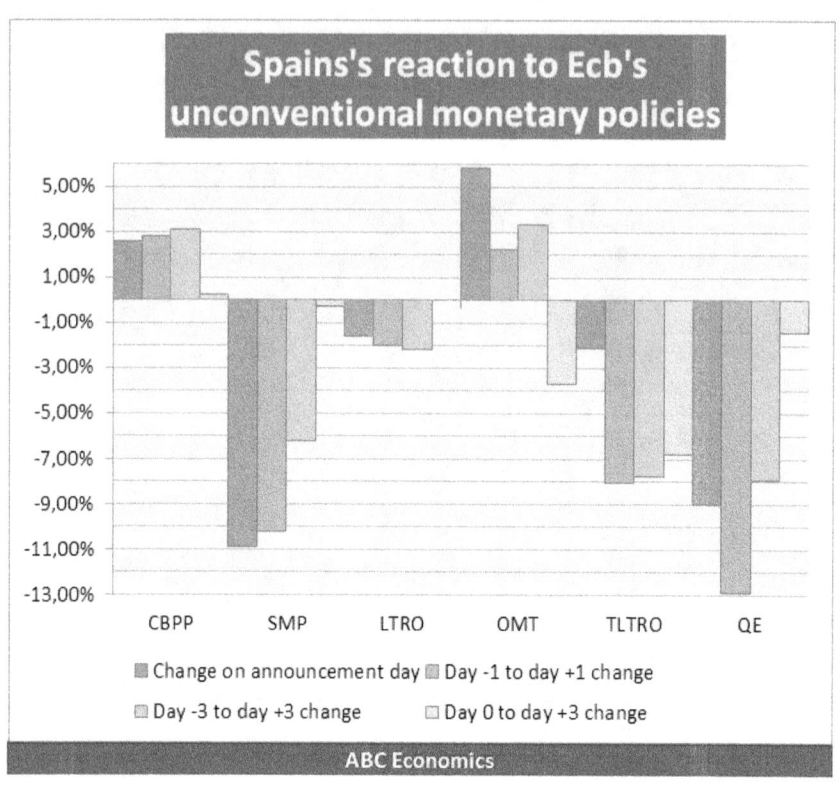

Inflation rate in the United Kingdom and Bank of England's Quantitative Easing programme announcements

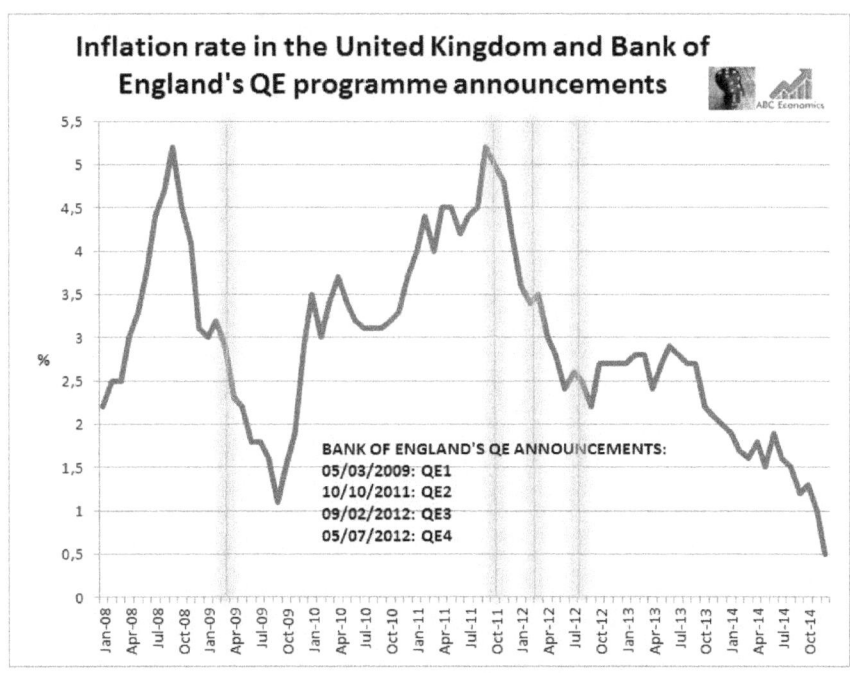

Sources: rateinflation.com and Bank of England

Inflation rate in the United States and Federal Reserve's Quantitative Easing programme announcements

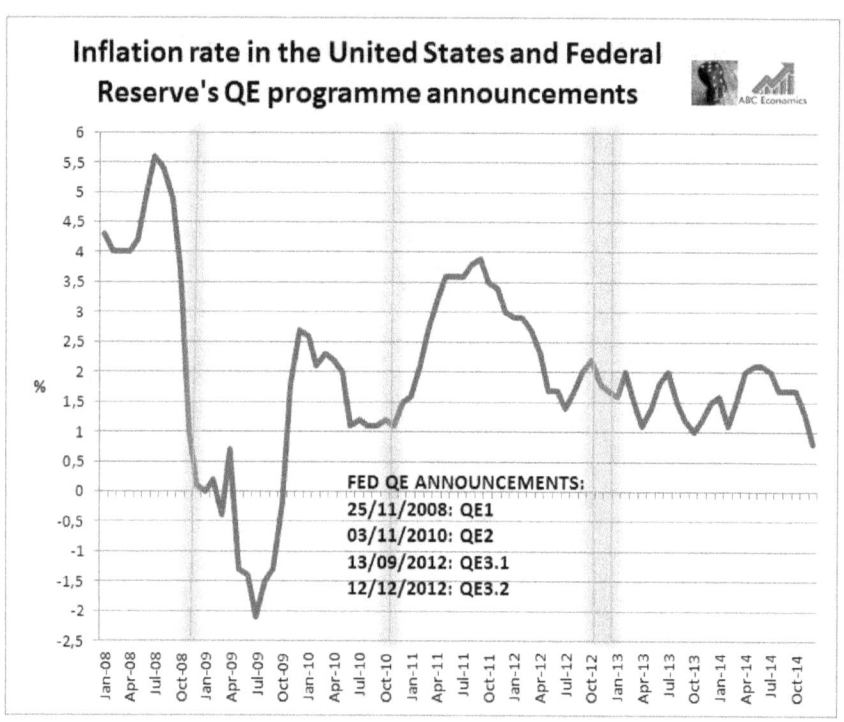

Sources: rateinflation.com and Federal Reserve

How will S&P and NASDAQ react to the FED's first interest rate increase since 2006?

The Federal Reserve is laying the groundwork for the first interest rate hike since 2006. Markets expect FED Chair Janet Yellen to increase rates above the current 0,00-0,25% level in the second half of the year provided that inflation returns to 2%. If the move is confirmed, the FED would be the first major central bank to increase rates since the subprime mortgages bubble burst.

Stanley Fischer, vice chair of the FED's board of governors and voting member on its policymaking committee, suggested that there is a "high probability" of a rate increase this year as the U.S. economy is "very close" to achieving a natural rate of unemployment and that inflation should rise as the effect of low oil wears off "in a couple months, so it's about time".

However, outside experts, including Nobel prize-winner Paul Krugman, have warned that high levels of debt among many US households would make an early rate rise risky. Nevertheless, a rate hike is expected at some stage in the near term.

In this chapter we estimate the financial markets reaction to the FED's announcements.

To do so, we observed all rate increase instances since 1995 where a rate increase was announced.

We examined 24 events in total from February 1995 to June 2006, and measured how the Standard & Poor's 500 (S&P 500), NASDAQ 100, NASDAQ BANK, NASDAQ

FED rate increases from 1995				
Event	Date	From	To	Change
E1	01/02/1995	5,50	6,00	0,50
E2	25/03/1997	5,25	5,50	0,25
E3	30/06/1999	4,75	5,00	0,25
E4	24/08/1999	5,00	5,25	0,25
E5	16/11/1999	5,25	5,50	0,25
E6	02/02/2000	5,50	5,75	0,25
E7	21/03/2000	5,75	6,00	0,25
E8	30/06/2004	1,00	1,25	0,25
E9	10/08/2004	1,25	1,50	0,25
E10	21/09/2004	1,50	1,75	0,25
E11	10/11/2004	1,75	2,00	0,25
E12	14/12/2004	2,00	2,25	0,25
E13	02/02/2005	2,25	2,50	0,25
E14	22/03/2005	2,50	2,75	0,25
E15	03/05/2005	2,75	3,00	0,25
E16	30/06/2005	3,00	3,25	0,25
E17	09/08/2005	3,25	3,50	0,25
E18	20/09/2005	3,50	3,75	0,25
E19	01/11/2005	3,75	4,00	0,25
E20	13/12/2005	4,00	4,25	0,25
E21	31/01/2006	4,25	4,50	0,25
E22	28/03/2006	4,50	4,75	0,25
E23	10/05/2006	4,75	5,00	0,25
E24	29/06/2006	5,00	5,25	0,25

INSURANCE indexes, in addition to the GBP/USD cross rate, reacted to the announcement of interest rate variation.

Main conclusions

Relative to the 1995-2006 period, on average the NASDAQ 100 outperforms the S&P 500 and the NASDAQ sub-indexes.

Within the dataset, we observed that interest rate increases generated higher positive variations in the years preceding the dot-com bubble burst.

On average, the NASDAQ 100 yield a +3,35% return over a 2-day horizon between February 1995 and March 2000. The average returns were non-significant (+0,02% overnight change) or negative (-0,22% 2-day horizon) post-2000. A similar pattern was found in the other indexes we examined.

In respect of the GBP/USD cross rate, a positive variation in the interest rate would generally lead to the appreciation of the UK Sterling against the US Dollar, with an average 2-day increase of 0,18% (0,26% pre-dotcom bubble and 0,14% thereafter).

Our 2015 prediction

ABC Economics agrees with Paul Krugman's assertion that an imminent rate increase would be premature as US inflation is yet to reach the FED's 2% target. However, should Janet Yellen go ahead and swiftly announce a 25 basis point hike, ABC Economics would expect the markets to yield null or negative returns over a two-day horizon.

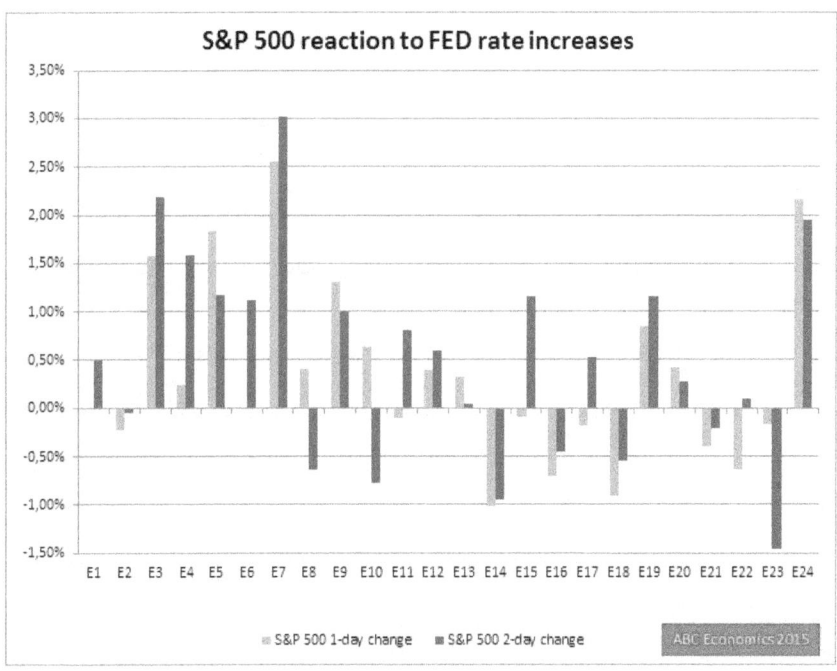

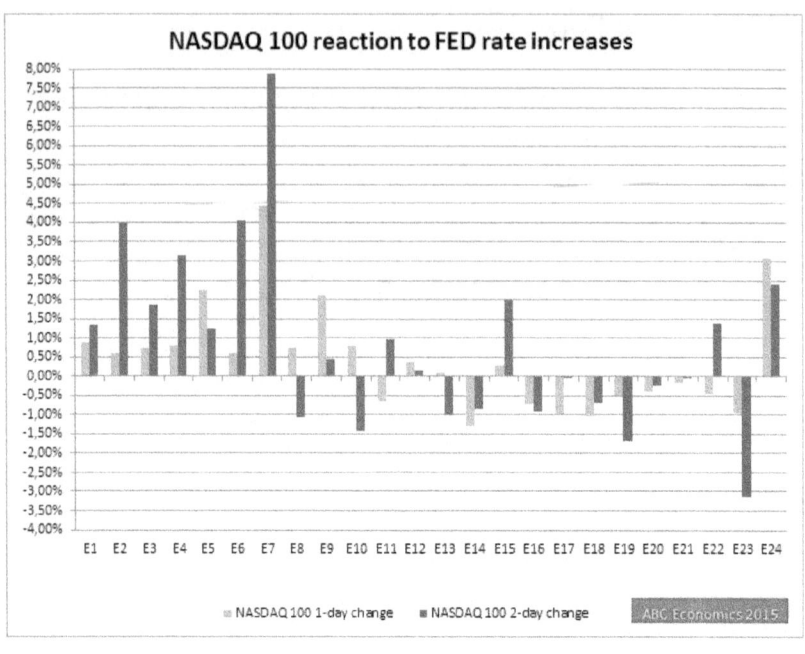
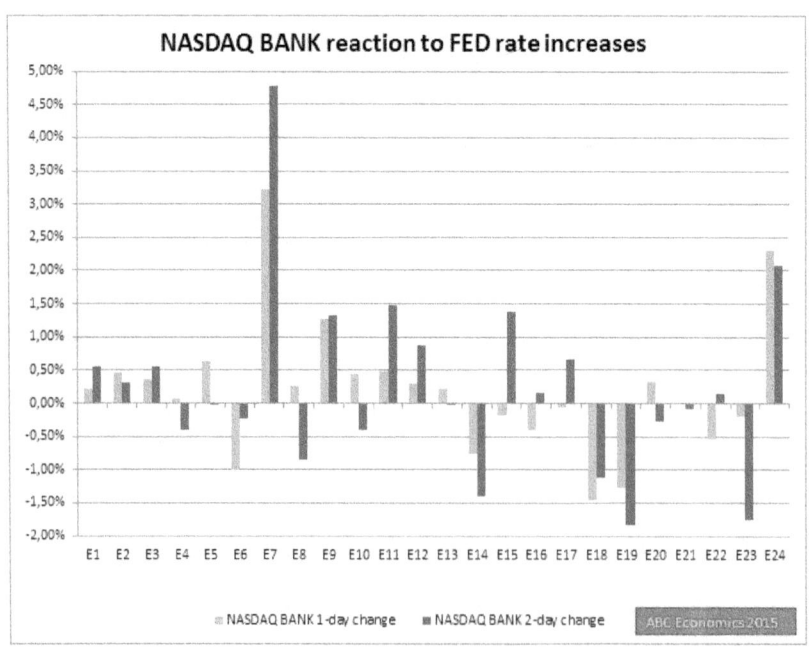

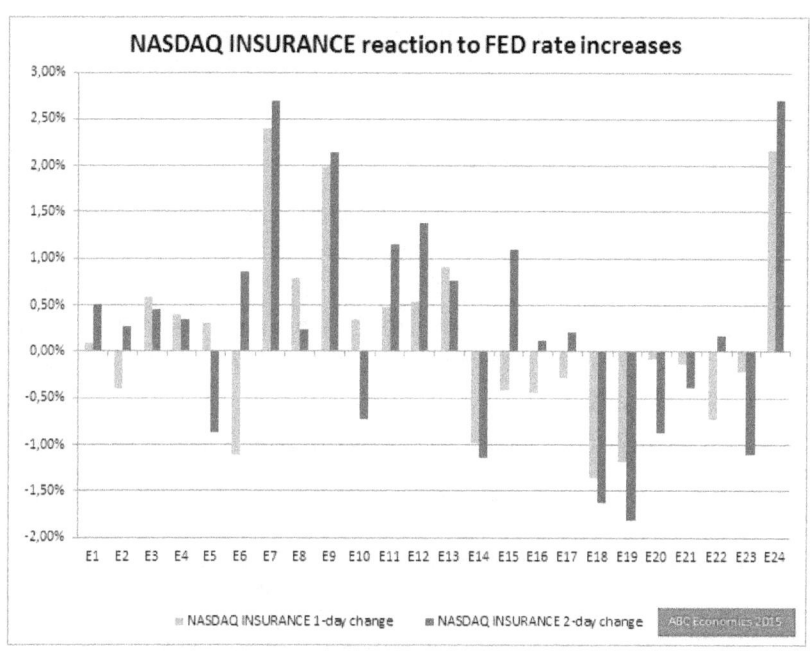
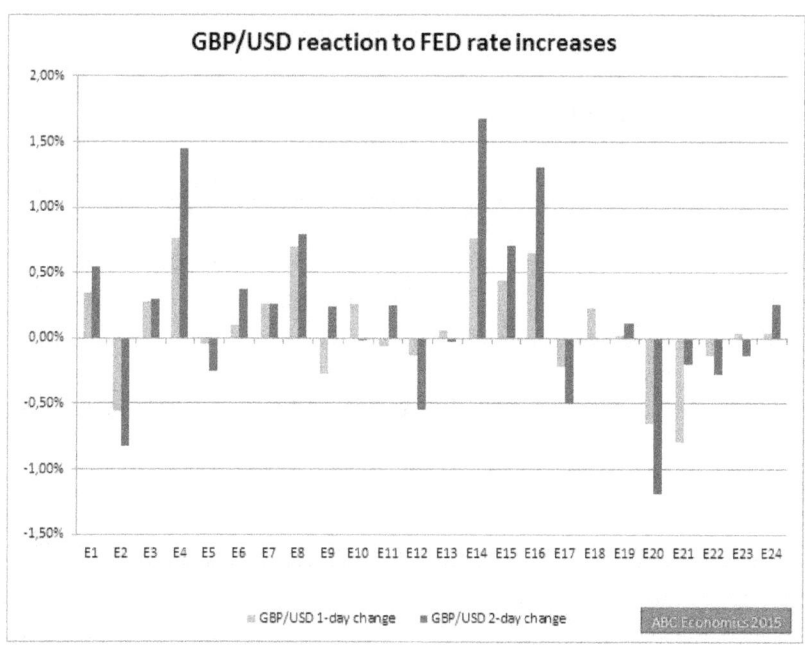

How markets will react to a new Greek bailout package?

On 18 February 2015 Greece's newly elected left-wing government requested an extension of the Master Financial Assistance Facility Agreement for Greece.

Following the agreement of the Eurogroup to extend the programme by four months, underpinned by the commitment of the Greek government to a comprehensive list of reforms and the completion of the national parliamentary procedures, the extension was finalised by a decision of the EFSF Board of Directors on 27 February.

The extension allows the Greek authorities to design and implement, in close coordination with the EC/ECB/IMF, reforms that should lead to a successful conclusion of the review and the design of the follow-up arrangements.

Research objectives and sampling

With the likelihood of a new programme to be negotiated in the near term, the research unit of ABC Economics investigated how the sovereign debt markets reacted to the announcement of the first two Greek bailout programmes on 2 May 2010 and on 14 March 2014.

Our sample includes the 10-year yields of the so-called GIIPS countries (Greece, Ireland, Italy, Portugal and Spain) in addition to the French and German sovereign papers.

2010 and 2012 Greek bailout programmes

First Economic Adjustment Programme for Greece

On 2 May 2010, the Eurogroup agreed to provide bilateral loans pooled by the European Commission (so-called "Greek Loan Facility" – GLF) for a total amount of €80 billion to be disbursed over the period May 2010 through June 2013. *(This amount was eventually reduced by €2.7 billion because Slovakia decided not to participate in the Greek Loan Facility Agreement while Ireland and Portugal stepped down from the facility as they requested financial assistance themselves).*

The financial assistance agreed by euro area Member States was part of a joint package, with the IMF committing additional €30 billion under a stand-by arrangement (SBA).

Second Economic Adjustment Programme for Greece

On 14 March 2012, euro area finance ministers approved financing of the Second Economic Adjustment Programme for Greece. The euro area Member States and the IMF committed the undisbursed amounts of the first programme (Greek Loan Facility) plus an additional €130 billion for the years 2012-14. Whereas the financing of the first programme was based on bilateral loans, it was agreed that – on the side of euro area Member States – the second programme would be financed by the European Financial Stability Facility (EFSF), which had been fully operational since August 2010.

In total, the second programme foresees financial assistance of €164.5 billion until the end of 2014. Of this amount, the euro area commitment amounts to €144.7 billion to be provided via the EFSF, while the IMF contributes €19.8 billion.

GIIPS and French spreads over 10-year German Bunds

In the case of the announcement of the first Greek bailout programme, over a 7-day horizon, spreads over the 10-year German sovereign paper increased across the entire sample, ranging from a low of +5 points for France to a high of +102 points for Greece.

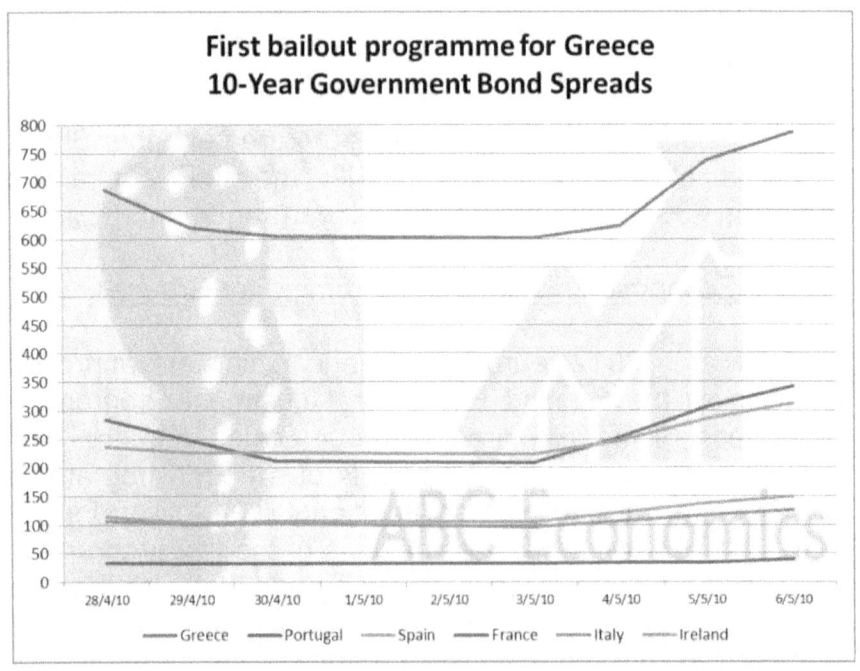

With regard to the second bailout package, spreads over the German bund decreased, ranging from -8 points for Spain to -43 points for the Portuguese sovereign paper. This was largely attributable to German yields increasing over the seven-day observation window (from 180 to 206 points).

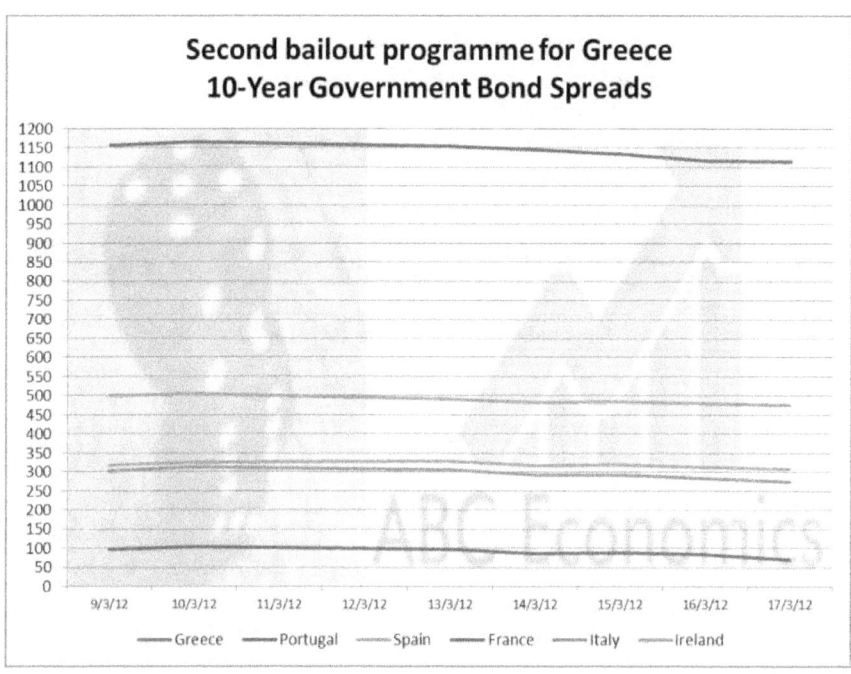

Note that in 2012 Greek yields were not available as Greece was temporarily forced to withdraw from the international bond markets.

Review of the 10-year yield performance for GIIPS, France and Germany

When the first bailout programme was announced, we observed that 10-year yields increased in Greece, Ireland, Portugal and Spain – countries which at the time were already feeling (or beginning to feel) the heat of the so-called sovereign debt crisis. By contrast, French and German yields decreased over the 7-day horizon.

The picture is less clear when we assess the sovereign debt market reaction to the announcement of the second bailout programme as German bunds rose sharply whilst – with the exception of Spanish sovereign papers – all other yields remained broadly unchanged.

ABC Economics	Change on announcement day	Change over a 3-day horizon	Change over a 7-day horizon
First bailout programme for Greece			
Germany	1,01%	-2,02%	-7,05%
Greece	0,00%	1,33%	8,23%
Portugal	0,00%	6,88%	6,36%
Spain	0,50%	2,23%	3,65%
France	0,91%	-1,22%	-4,82%
Italy	-0,50%	-0,25%	-0,50%
Ireland	0,00%	2,87%	10,09%
Second bailout programme for Greece			
Germany	7,69%	8,24%	14,44%
Greece	N/A	N/A	N/A
Portugal	0,37%	-0,37%	-1,27%
Spain	0,59%	1,37%	3,62%
France	1,08%	2,51%	-0,36%
Italy	0,00%	0,20%	0,00%
Ireland	0,59%	1,19%	0,44%

Bailouts, spreads and yields in Germany, France and PIIGS

Having previously observed the sovereign debt market reaction to the announcement of Greece's bailout programmes, we now switch our focus to the EU financial assistance granted to three of the so called "peripheral Member States" of the eurozone: Ireland (who joined the EU aid programme in 2010), Portugal (2011) and Cyprus (2013).

Brief overview of the bailout programmes

2010 Economic Adjustment Programme for Ireland

The Economic Adjustment Programme for Ireland was formally agreed in December 2010. It included a joint financing package of €85 billion for the period 2010-2013.

This was based on contributions from the EFSM (€22.5 billion), the EFSF (€17.7 billion), bilateral contributions from the United Kingdom (€3.8 billion), Sweden (€0.6 billion) and Denmark (€0.4 billion) as well as funding from the IMF (€22.5 billion). Moreover, there was an Irish contribution through the Treasury cash buffer and investments of the National Pension Reserve Funds.

2011 Portuguese bailout

On 7 April 2011 Portugal requested financial assistance from the EU, the eurozone Member States and the International Monetary Fund (IMF). An Economic Adjustment Programme was negotiated in May 2011 between the Portuguese authorities and officials from the European Commission (EC), the European Central Bank (ECB) and the IMF.

The agreement on the Programme was formally adopted on 17 May 2011 at the Eurogroup/ECOFIN meeting in Brussels. The Memorandum of Understanding and the Loan Agreement were signed thereafter. It covered the period 2011 to mid-2014 and included a joint financing package of €78 billion, €26 billion of which provided by the EU/EFSM, €26 billion by the EFSF and about €26 billion provided by the IMF.

The Programme contained reforms to promote growth and jobs, fiscal measures to reduce the public debt and deficit, and measures to ensure the stability of the country's financial sector.

2013 Economic Adjustment Programme for Cyprus

Following a request by Cyprus on 25 June 2012, the European Commission (EC), the European Central Bank (ECB) and the International Monetary Fund (IMF) agreed an Economic Adjustment Programme with the Cypriot authorities on 2 April 2013.

The Programme was agreed by the eurozone Member States on 24 April 2013 and by the IMF Board on 15 May 2013. It covers the period 2013-2016. The financial package will cover up to €10 billion; the ESM will provide up to €9 billion, and the International Monetary Fund (IMF) is expected to contribute around €1 billion.

Research objectives and sampling

In order to assess the sovereign bond market response to the announcement of the above-mentioned bailout programmes, we opted to include within our sample the 10-year yields of the so-called GIIPS countries (Greece, Ireland,

Italy, Portugal and Spain) in addition to the French and German sovereign papers.

Main conclusions

In the case of the Irish bailout, on the basis of a 7-day horizon, spreads over the 10-year German sovereign paper remained broadly consistent – ranging from a low of -3 points for Spain to a high of +47 points for Greece – with the sole exception of Ireland (+83 points over the estimation window).

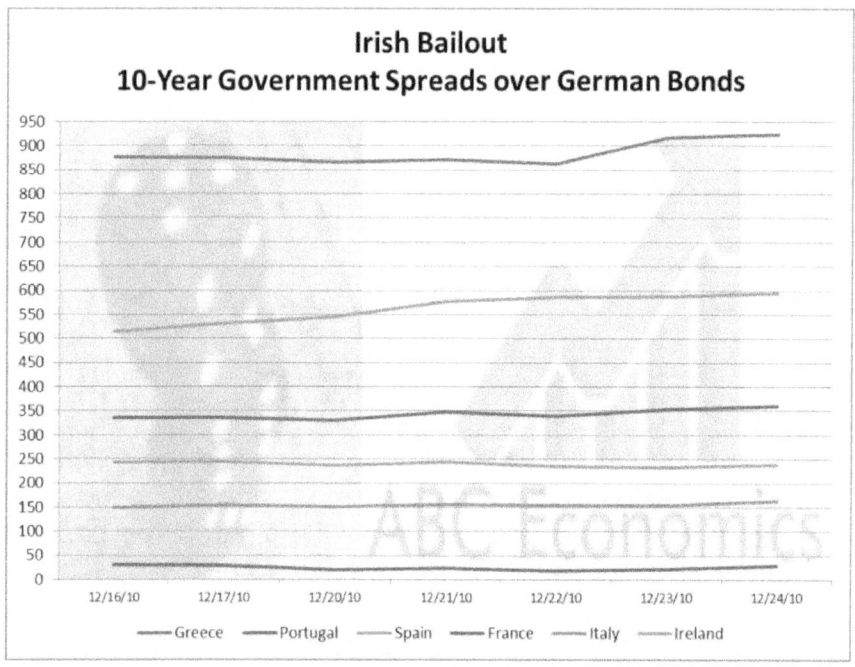

A similar pattern was observed when the Eurogroup agreed Portugal's financial assistance package with spreads over the German bund remaining vastly unchanged (movements ranged from +4 point for France to +24 for Irish government papers), the sole exception being Greece (104 points increase over the seven day spectrum).

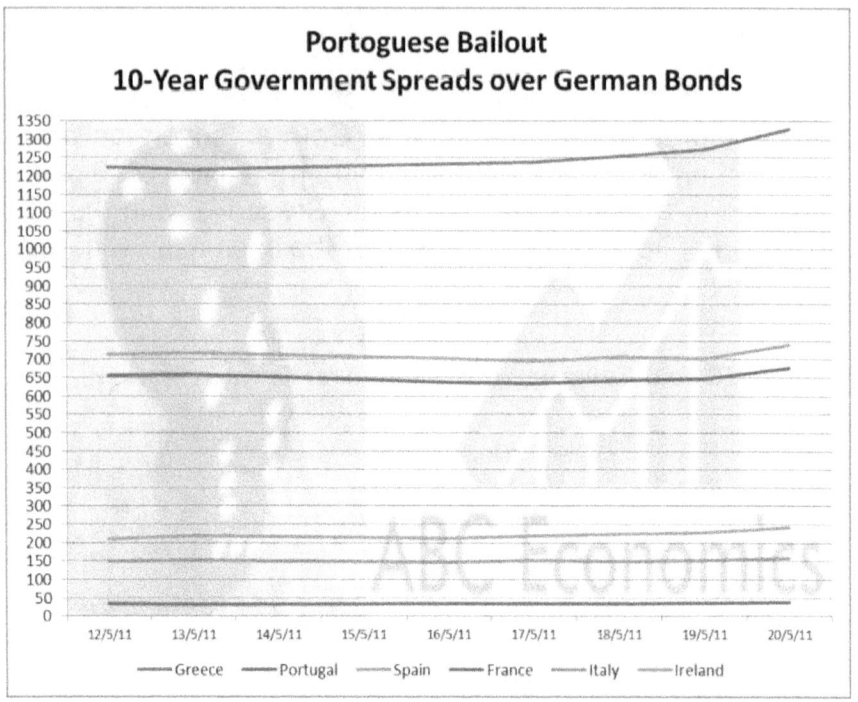

The sovereign debt markets warmly welcomed the rescue of Cyprus as spreads over the German 10-year bonds fell across the entire sample peaking -41 points in the case of the Spanish emissions.

As noted in the table below, over a 7-day horizon, government bonds yields decreased within the core members of the eurozone, namely France and Germany, and rose elsewhere within peripheral Europe.

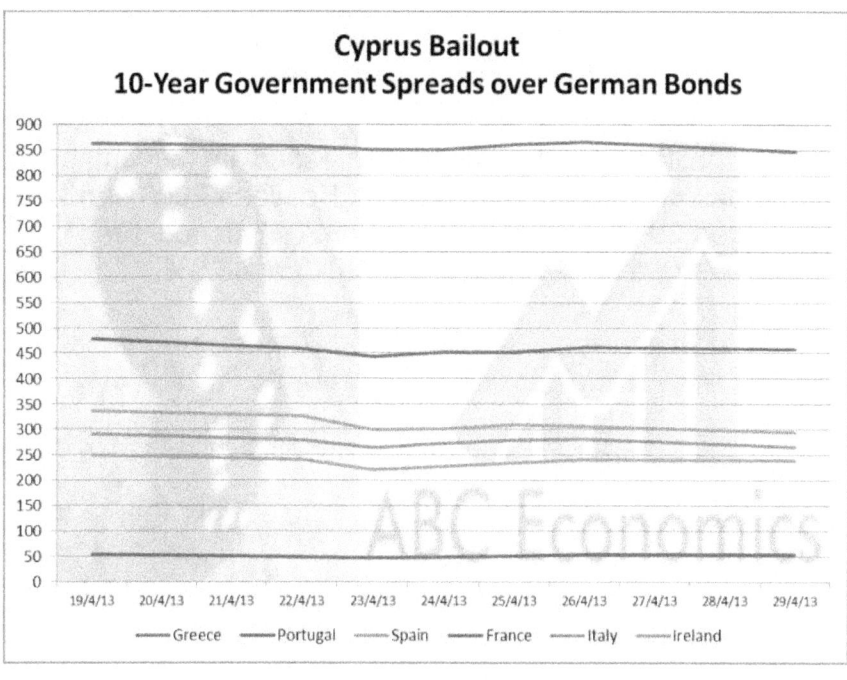

Change on announcement day							
Bailout event / 10 Yr Gov. Yield	Germany	Greece	Portugal	Spain	France	Italy	Ireland
CYPRUS	2,34%	-2,66%	1,60%	-2,18%	0,00%	-2,35%	N/A
IRELAND	0,68%	0,08%	2,49%	0,91%	0,30%	0,43%	3,26%
PORTUGAL	-0,96%	0,06%	-0,53%	0,95%	-0,87%	0,00%	-0,99%

Change over a 3-day horizon							
Bailout event / 10 Yr Gov. Yield	Germany	Greece	Portugal	Spain	France	Italy	Ireland
CYPRUS	0,78%	-4,40%	0,16%	-2,57%	-1,49%	-2,99%	N/A
IRELAND	-0,34%	-0,34%	1,56%	-0,36%	-0,30%	0,65%	4,66%
PORTUGAL	0,00%	1,36%	0,63%	2,10%	0,00%	0,43%	0,30%

Change over a 7-day horizon							
Bailout event / 10 Yr Gov. Yield	Germany	Greece	Portugal	Spain	France	Italy	Ireland
CYPRUS	-5,47%	-3,39%	0,48%	-5,73%	-13,37%	-7,69%	N/A
IRELAND	-2,93%	3,54%	3,10%	-1,45%	-2,05%	1,96%	9,22%
PORTUGAL	-1,61%	6,45%	1,66%	5,18%	-0,29%	1,30%	1,85%

Italy's tax burden and government Revenue since 2000

In Italy the total tax burden – expressed in percentage of GDP – has progressively increased. Between 2000 and 2006 it averaged 39.8%, whilst in the 2007-2013 period it recorded an average rate of 42% peaking in 2013 at 43.3%.

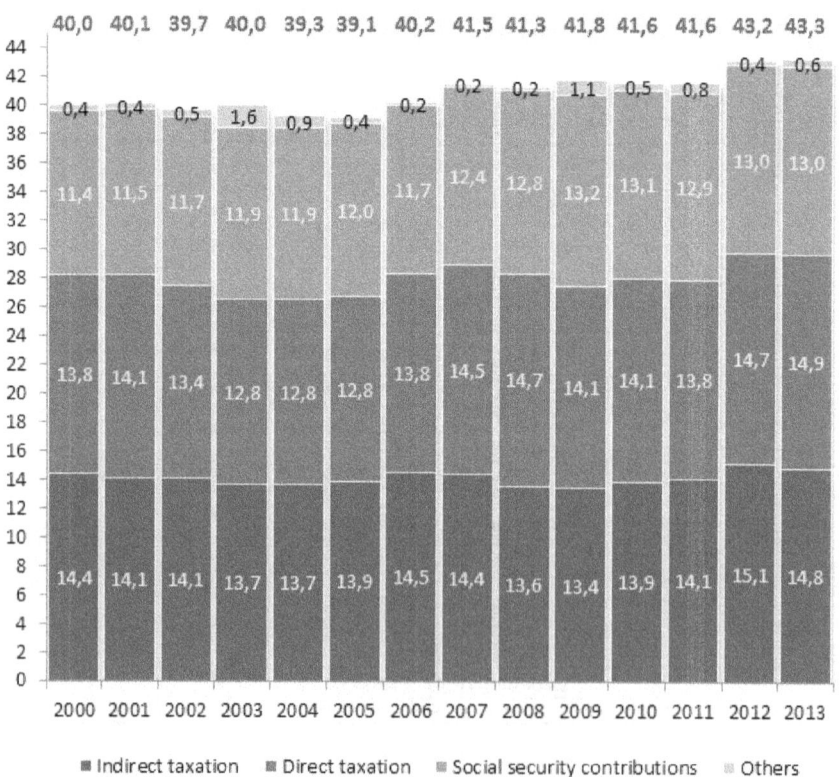

From the ABC Economics infographic analysis reported below, the reader will also observe that both the year-on-year and cumulative changes in government revenue and tax burden rates have recorded similar movements.

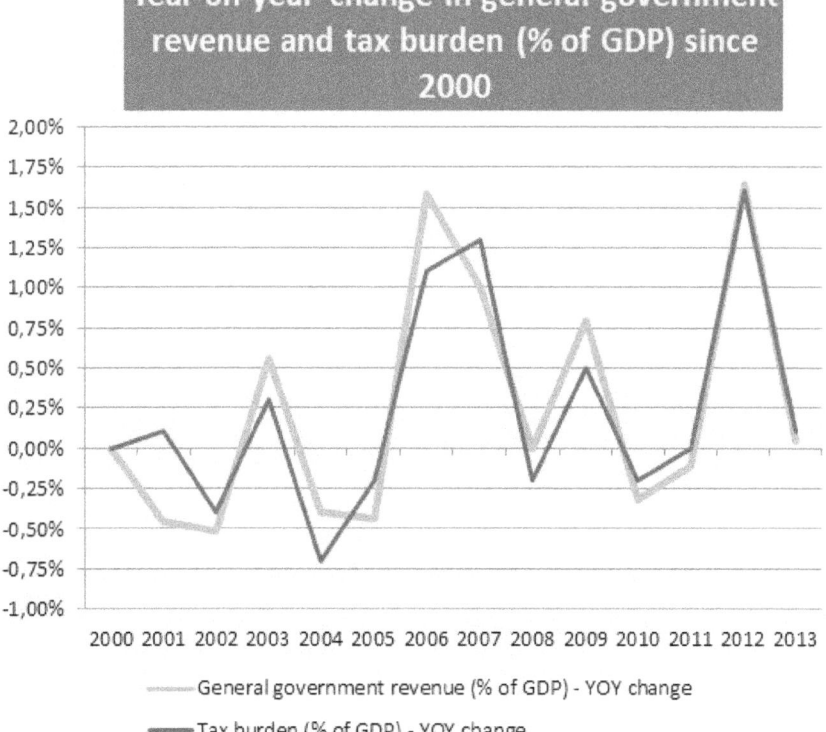

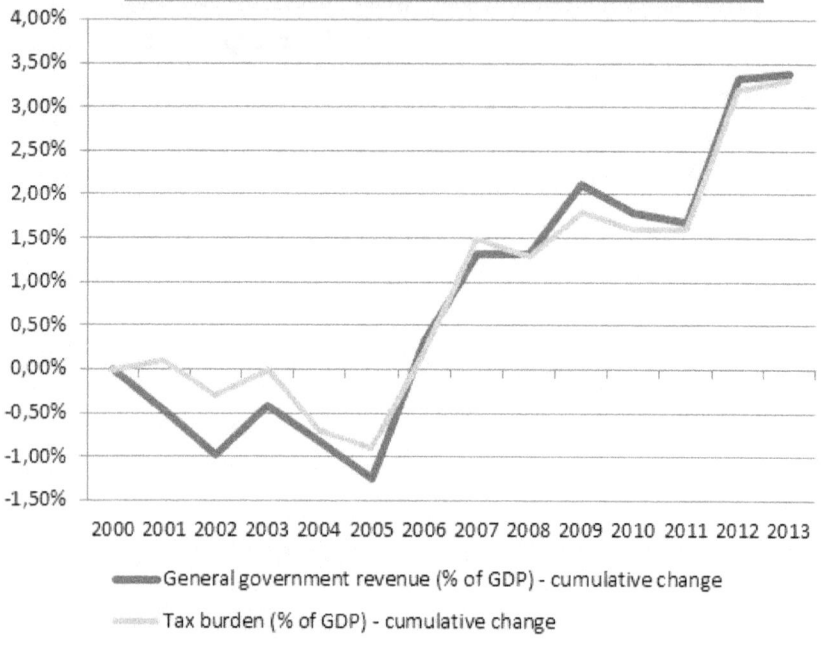

Europe's tax revenues as a percentage of GDP (2000-2013)

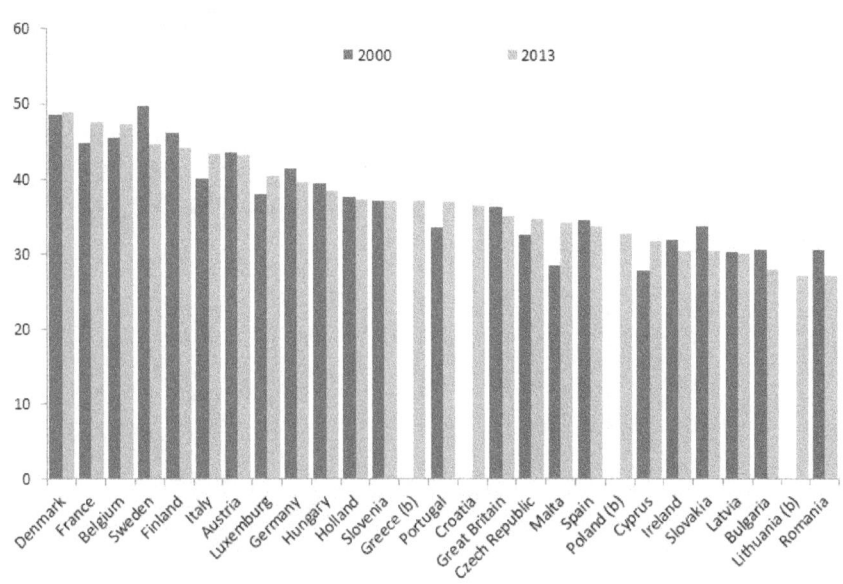

Source: EU Commission

(a) Data as at November 2014
(b) Data for the year 2000 not available
(c) Estonia and EU28 data for 2000 and 2013 not available

TARGET2 imbalances

This chapter reports looks at the infamous TARGET2 imbalances, which are yet another symptom of the ongoing malaise in the eurozone.

The key to understanding the functioning of the TARGET2 mechanism is to look at the "truck purchase" example reported below which will assist us in understanding how the central bank balance sheets work.

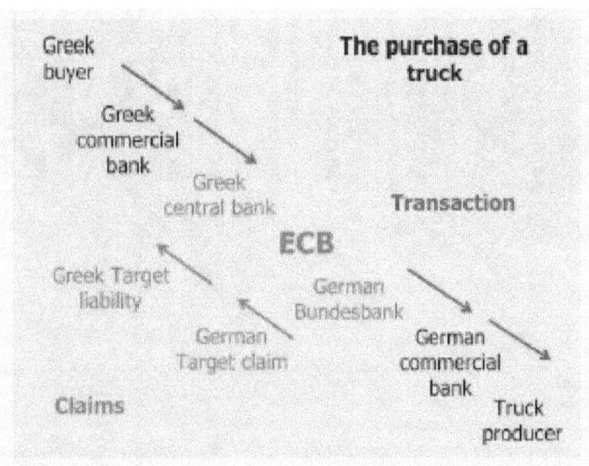

In this example the Greek central bank has to reduce "base money" while Bundesbank increases "base money" by transferring cash from the Greek banking system to the German banking system (to pay for the truck). Simultaneously Bundesbank now has a future claim on the ECB while the ECB has a claim on the Greek central bank (effectively to reverse the "cash transfer" in the future). With significant periphery trade deficits, these claims have now grown quite large.

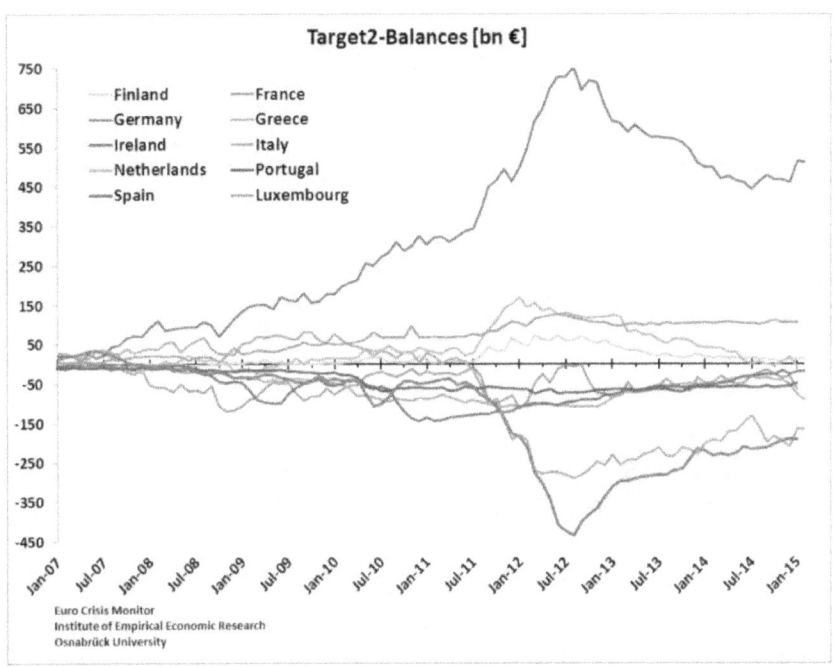

The concern around TARGET2 imbalances is that central banks owe a great deal of money to each other via the ECB and should a nation drop out of the eurozone, these liabilities may not be met. The ECB may then have to take a large loss. A mechanism for a nation's exit from the euro area was never developed.

What do financial markets know about terrorism?

The purpose of this brief research is to test the following hypothesis:

> *Market movers are able to predict the occurrence of terrorist acts*

To test this hypothesis we selected:

Three variables: one "independent" variable (the VIX Index) and two "control" variables (Gold and Brent Oil)

An event window of 7 days (day -5 to day +1) covering five trading days prior to the event, the actual event day, and the first subsequent trading day.

Observed events

- 13 November 2015: Paris Attacks
- 7 January 2015: Charlie Hebdo Shootings, Paris
- 7 July 2005: London Bombings
- 11 March 2004: Madrid Train Bombing
- 11 September 2001: World Trade Centre, New York

The variables

Independent variable – VIX is a trademarked ticker symbol for the CBOE Volatility Index, a popular measure of the implied volatility of S&P 500 index options; the VIX is calculated by the Chicago Board Options Exchange (CBOE). Often referred to as the fear index or the fear gauge, the VIX represents one measure of the market's expectation of stock market volatility over the next 30-day period.

Control variables – Gold and Brent Oil are two commodities which are usually looked at in times of financial or geopolitical stress, with the former being a 'safe haven' investment and the latter a geopolitical thermometer.

Results and conclusions

As previously noted, VIX is intended to be a forward-looking index, predominantly focussing on US stocks. However, the author of this research observed the following:

- in all the instances the Index increased in the 5 trading days prior to the terrorist event i.e. the VIX closing value on day -5 is always lower than the close on the day of the event;
- with the except of 9/11, the VIX Index closed lower on the day following the attacks;
- on 9/11 the VIX did not trade as the attacks struck the Twin Towers before the Chicago Stock Exchange opened. Additionally, normal trading activity did not resume until 17 September 2001.

In order to test the above we then considered the control variables. If Gold and Brent Oil show consistent patterns ahead of terrorist attacks i.e. they generally either increase or decrease before a given event, then we would be able to unravel evidence to support the view that market movers were warned ahead of the events.

However, as far as pricing is concerned, our analysis did not highlight any consistent behaviour or anything unusual at all over the selected time-horizon. Therefore, on that basis we conclude that the VIX Index rose by chance and no causal effects were found.

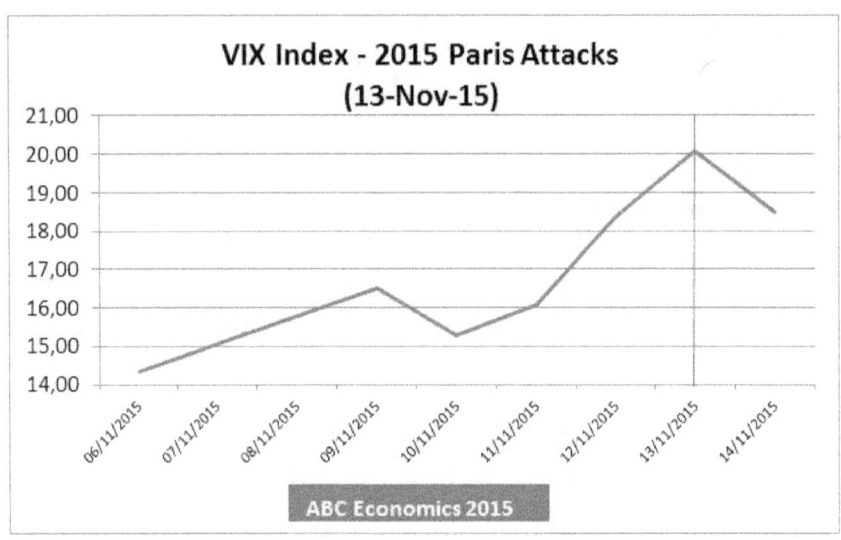

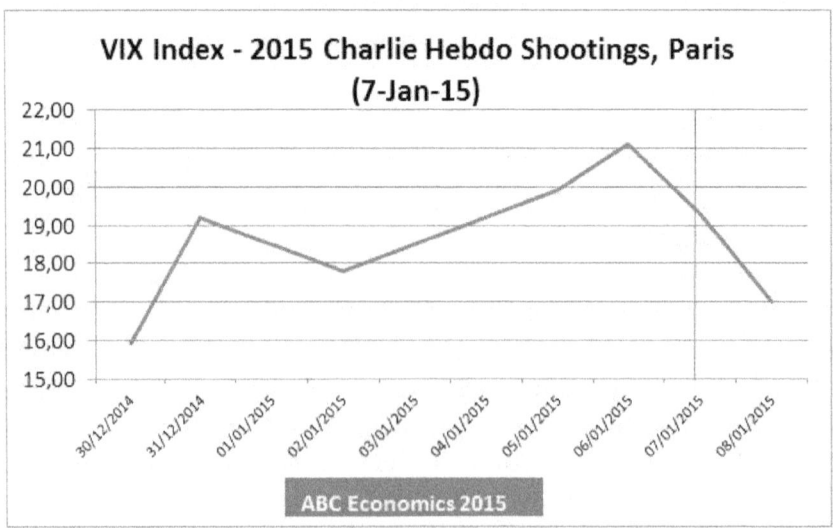

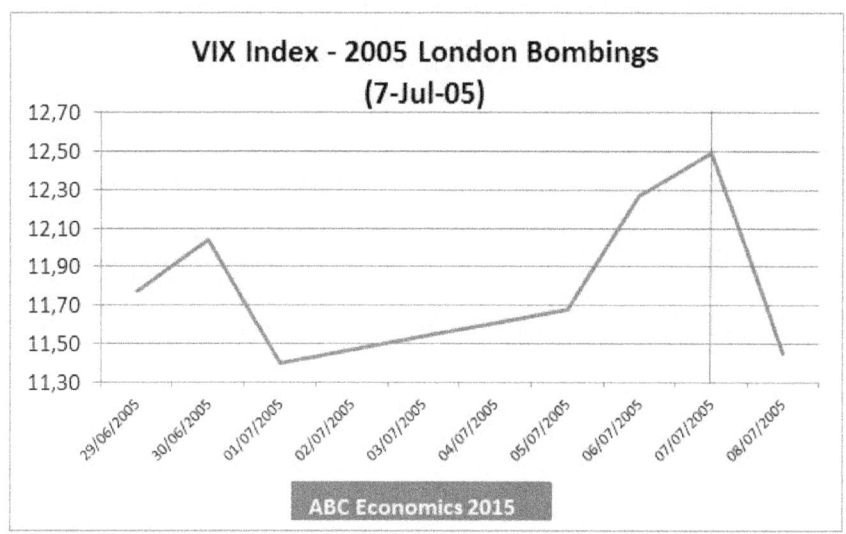
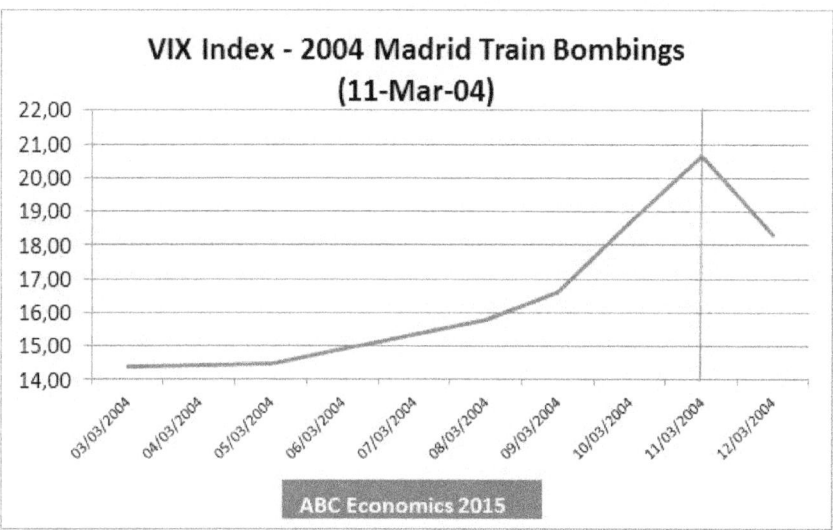

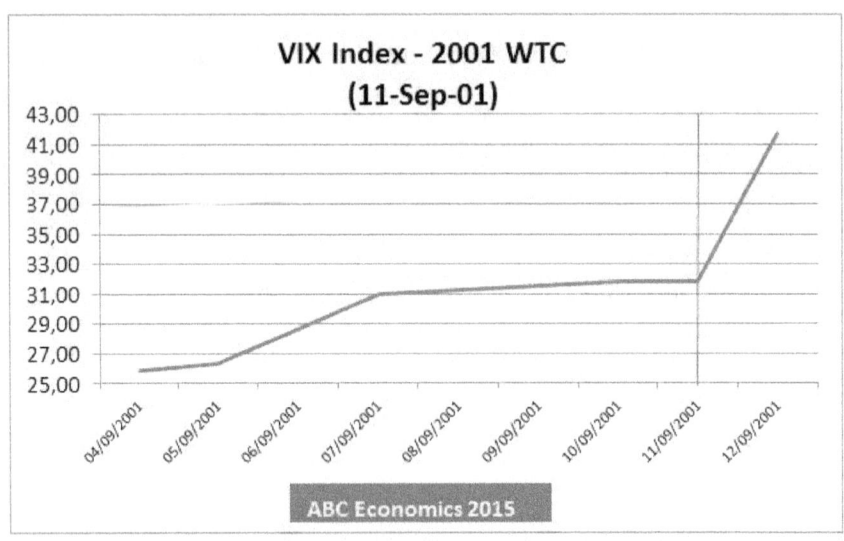
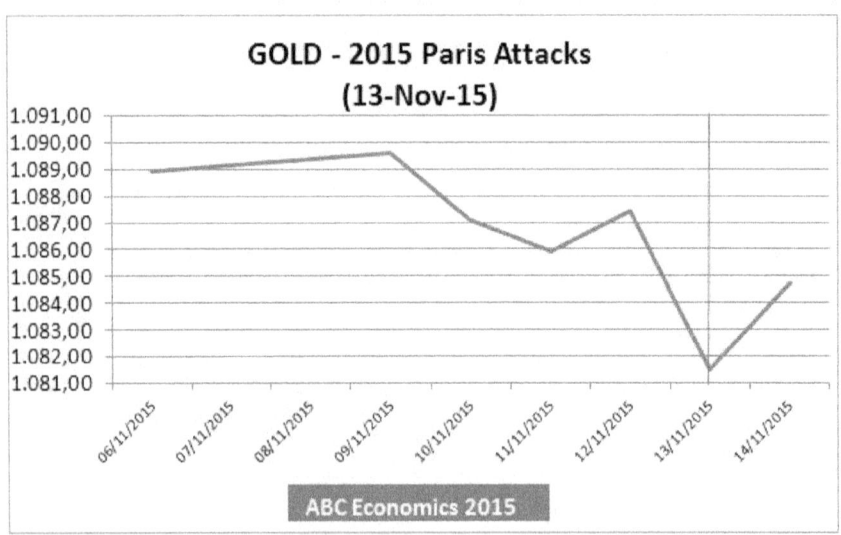

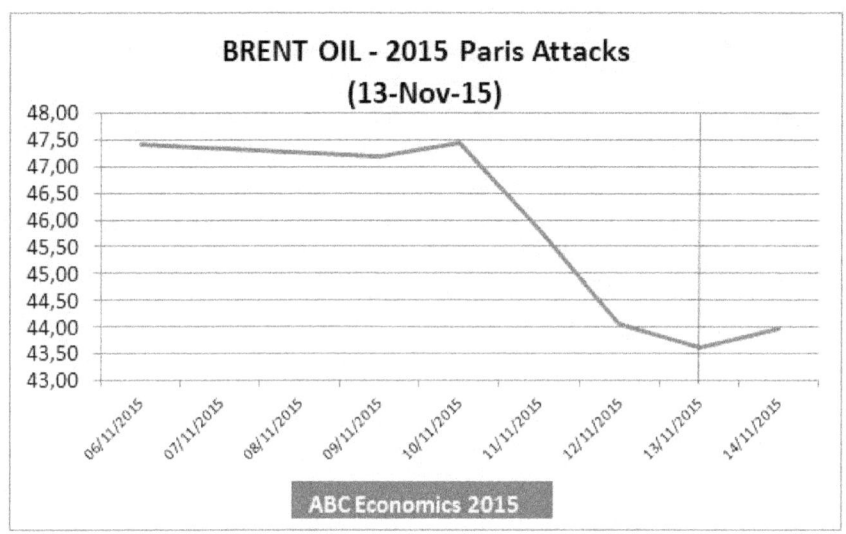

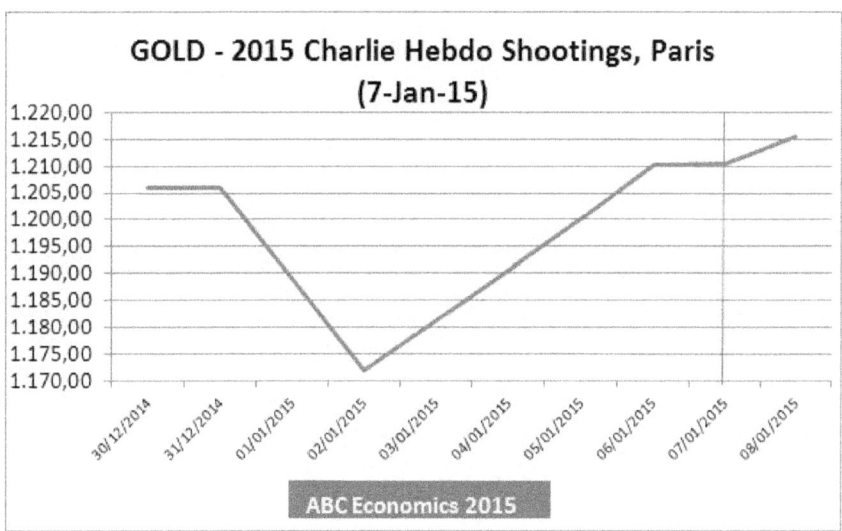

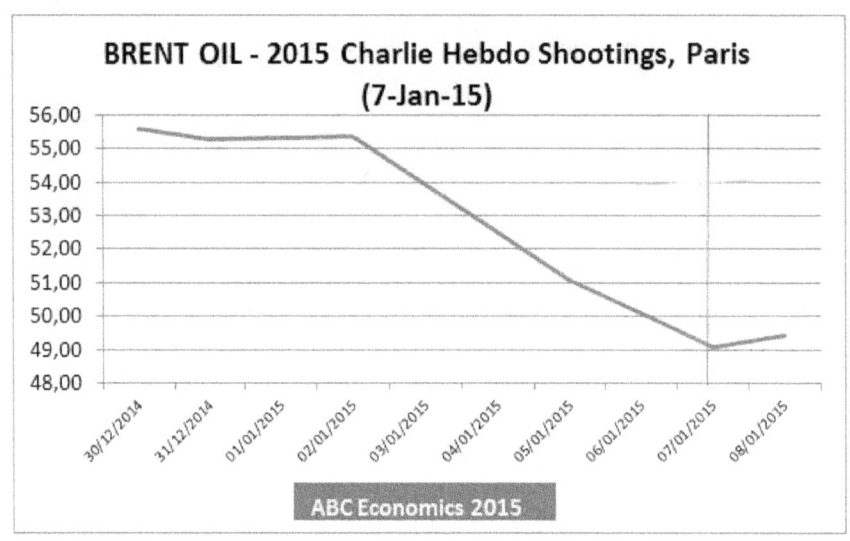
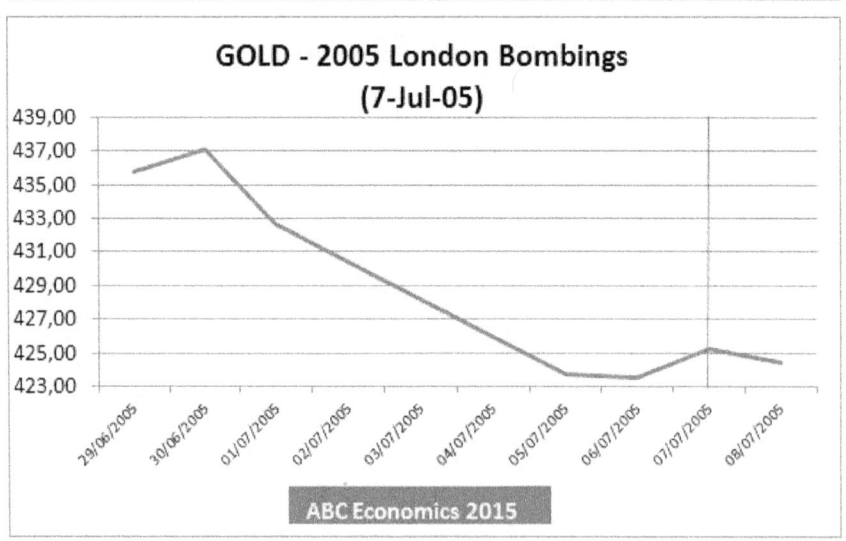

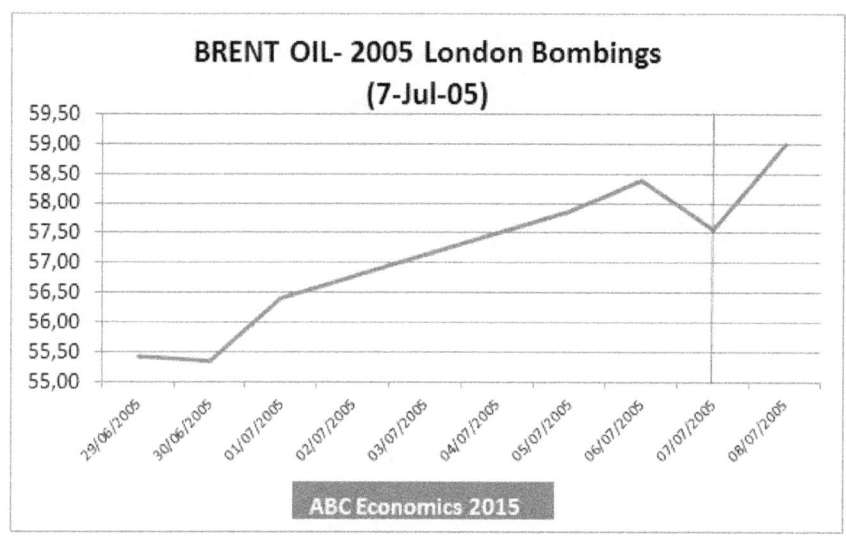
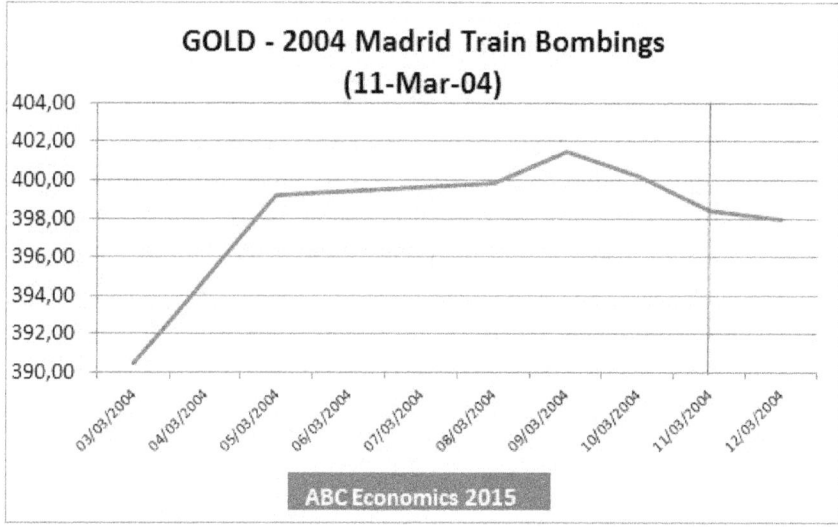

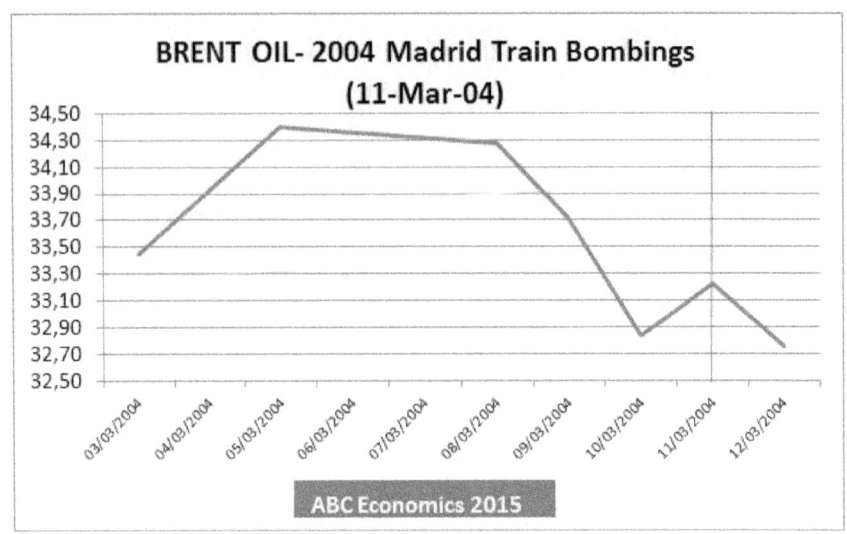

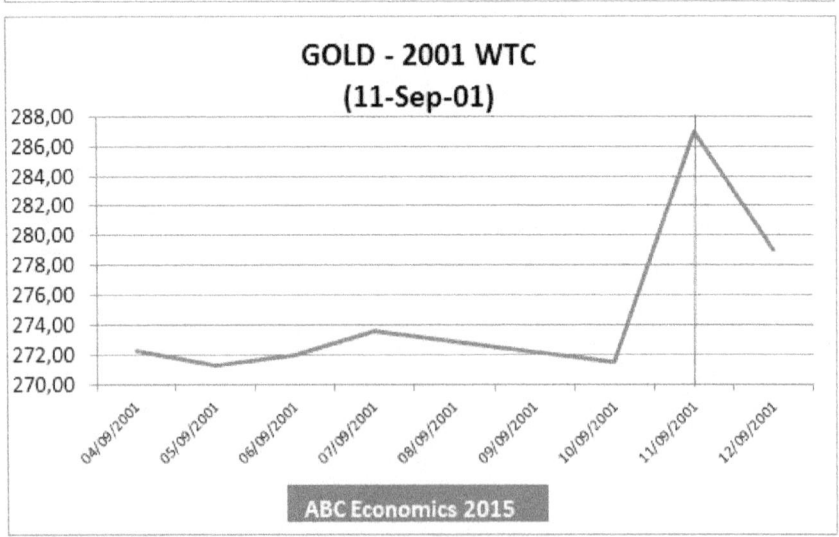

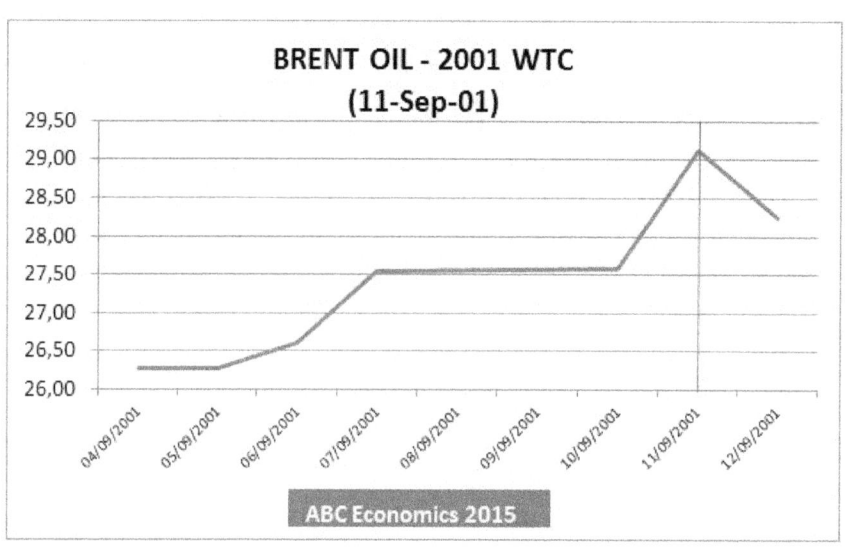

Sources

This book is entirely based on secondary data which was collected by third parties; reviewed, analysed and reworked by the author. Third party sources include the following:

ABC Economics
Bank of England
Bloomberg
Borsa Italiana
CNBC
EU Commission
Euro Crisis Monitor
European Central Bank
Federal Reserve
International Monetary Fund
Istat
Library of Economics and Liberty
Mediobanca Securities
Place du Luxembourg
Quandl
Rate Inflation
Sober Look
The Financial Times
The Guardian
Treccani
VOX - CEPR
Yahoo! Finance

Acknowledgements

The author would like to thank:

Alessandra Fugazzi
Antonio Guglielmi
Carlo Signani
Christina Tonini
Filippo Baglini
John Wood
London School of Journalism
Luigi Patisso
Michael Smurfit Graduate School of Business
Nicola Spanu
Peter McNamara

ABC Economics – Abbiamo Bisogno di Crescita

Website: http://abceconomics.com/

Email: abc.economics@yahoo.com

Facebook: https://www.facebook.com/abceconomics

Twitter: https://twitter.com/ABCEconomics

ABC Economics has been cited on several occasions by the media, making a splash on the front pages of Il Sole 24 Ore and Il Giornale, mentioned by Otto e Mezzo (a TV programme) and by a handful of Italian blogs, in addition to Wikipedia and a number of US news portals e.g. Zero Hedge, TV channels and UK radio stations. Additionally, some of our ABC Economics work was translated into and reported by French and Russian news portals.

We are independent. We do not receive any public funding.

"**IDEE PER L'ITALIA: Abbattere il debito pubblico per restituire allo Stato la sovranità in politica economica**" (ISBN 9781291426281)

"**A.B.C. ITALIA (Abbiamo Bisogno di Crescita)**" (ISBN 9781291943238)

"**BREXIT?**" (ISBN 9781326311742)

Copyright © 2016 Stefano Fugazzi

http://abceconomics.com/